Tackling Tough Interview
Questions
In A Week

Alison Straw is an independent consultant and executive coach. Her career has been devoted to helping individuals, groups and organizations develop. She is passionate about engaging and inspiring people and has worked with many senior executives, supporting them in developing themselves, their careers and their organizations. She has co-authored *Succeeding at Interviews* and *Successful Networking*.

Mo Shapiro, partner at INFORM T&C, is a master practitioner in NLP and coaching. She has an outstanding record as a communications and presentation skills coach and trainer and an international public speaker. Mo contributes regularly to all broadcast media, has authored *Successful Interviewing* and *Neuro-linguistic Programming* and co-authored *Succeeding at Interviews*.

Tackling Tough Interview Questions In A Week

Alison Straw and
Mo Shapiro

First published in Great Britain in 1999 by Hodder Education. An Hachette UK company.

This edition published in 2016 by John Murray Learning.

Copyright © Alison Straw and Mo Shapiro 1999, 2002, 2012, 2016

The right of Alison Straw and Mo Shapiro to be identified as the Authors of the Work has been asserted by them in accordance with the Copyright, Designs and Patents Act 1988.

Database right Hodder & Stoughton (makers)

The *Teach Yourself* name is a registered trademark of Hachette UK.

British Library Cataloguing in Publication Data: a catalogue record for this title is available from the British Library.

Library of Congress Catalog Card Number: on file.

Paperback ISBN 978 1 473 61036 1

eBook ISBN 978 1 444 15903 5

2

The publisher has used its best endeavours to ensure that any website addresses referred to in this book are correct and active at the time of going to press. However, the publisher and the author have no responsibility for the websites and can make no guarantee that a site will remain live or that the content will remain relevant, decent or appropriate.

The publisher has made every effort to mark as such all words which it believes to be trademarks. The publisher should also like to make it clear that the presence of a word in the book, whether marked or unmarked, in no way affects its legal status as a trademark.

Every reasonable effort has been made by the publisher to trace the copyright holders of material in this book. Any errors or omissions should be notified in writing to the publisher, who will endeavour to rectify the situation for any reprints and future editions.

Typeset by Cenveo® Publisher Services.

Printed and bound in Great Britain by CPI Group (UK) Ltd, Croydon, CR0 4YY.

John Murray Learning policy is to use papers that are natural, renewable and recyclable products and made from wood grown in sustainable forests. The logging and manufacturing processes are expected to conform to the environmental regulations of the country of origin.

John Murray Learning
Carmelite House
50 Victoria Embankment
London
EC4Y 0DZ
www.hodder.co.uk

Contents

Introduction

Tackling Tough Interview Questions In A Week was developed in response to readers wanting specific help in answering what they thought were tough interview questions. Since writing the first edition of the book, we have been challenged by individuals and situations that have made us stop and consider why people find questions tough and how to best prepare readers for these questions. We have continued to talk to people who have succeeded at interviews (some as a result of reading the book), and consulted colleagues who regularly interview. All this accumulated knowledge and experience is contained in this book.

Throughout the week, we will look at how to answer what many people consider to be the toughest interview questions. A question is often seen as tough because it's something you feel uncomfortable about – a career choice you made that you don't feel proud of; a missing qualification; redundancy or a business failure or simply that your career hasn't quite developed as you thought it would. Our advice is to analyse your past interview performance and, in going through the book, see which other questions you may find difficult. The formula is then simple – create a positive reply. Many people throughout their careers make mistakes – the challenge for all of us is to recover and to not let them hold us back.

By the end of the week, you should feel better informed about the process – the content, style and motivations behind questions – as well as feeling more confident about presenting your experience, your knowledge, your skills and your abilities.

We would like you to think of this book as your companion and guide through what can be uncharted waters. Your challenge is to apply this learning to yourself and the situations you face. Use the examples to develop a language and method of talking about yourself. Practise talking about yourself and this, together with your examples, will lead to easy, flowing answers that you can access even under pressure and from there to a successful job offer.

Remember that your interviewer is interested in you, not what you think is the 'right' answer. Many interviewers are becoming wise to, and wary of, 'textbook' answers. It is important to create responses that will differentiate you from the other candidates and hold the interviewer's attention.

The week is built on the themes of the tough questions you've told us you've faced at interview. We'd encourage you to go through the book day by day over the course of a week and create your own responses based on our advice. Each day covers a different theme:

- **Sunday** summarizes what an interview involves.
- **Monday** covers the opening stages of the interview and how to present yourself.
- **Tuesday** focuses on the main part of the interview where you have to convince the interviewer that you can do the job.
- **Wednesday** looks at how to answer more detailed questions about your background and skills.
- **Thursday** covers questions about how you would do the job.
- **Friday** looks at questions about how you would fit into the organization.
- **Saturday** gives advice on how to prepare and build your confidence before an interview.

At the end of each day there are some multiple-choice questions for you to check your understanding. By Saturday, you should have a healthy portfolio of answers to produce at any interview.

We hope you enjoy the book and that it helps you in your preparation for your interview and leads to success in getting the job you want.

**Alison Straw and
Mo Shapiro**

SUNDAY

What's involved?

Today is all about getting you ready for the early stages of the interview process, so that you are prepared and ready to make a good impression from the start. We will set the scene and help you understand what comes before the final face to face interview. Other books in this series help you focus on how to get an interview. Throughout the application process, you should be demonstrating how your skills and abilities fit with the organization and the role. This part of the recruitment process is often impersonal – it's about how you sell yourself on paper or online. As soon as you have been shortlisted, the process becomes very personal.

Evidence suggests that a bad recruitment decision is costly to the organization and, from your perspective, if the role, organization or expectations don't fit it can be costly for you too. Our experience suggests that a wrong career move can affect your confidence, self-esteem and even make you think differently about your career. It's important to recognize that wrong moves can be put right and the quicker you recognize this as a wrong move the better; the action to put it right might take a little longer.

Every organization or recruiter will have their own methods but we find that there are some core components you are likely to encounter on your journey to the interview. We will work through the following:

- Understanding interview objectives
- First steps
- Telephone screening
- Elements of the interview
- What makes a question tough?

Understanding interview objectives

It is amazing how many interviewees expect the interviewer to be so in charge of the interview that they disempower themselves by not having their own clear plan and set of objectives. Throughout the week, we will give you the opportunity to reflect on the reasoning behind the different kinds of questions you are asked. You will be able to consider your own aims. If you don't know what you want from a job, how will you know when you achieve it?

Today's objectives relate to overall considerations of what's involved for both parties in preparation for the interview itself.

The interviewer's objectives	The interviewee's objectives
To get the right person for the job with:	To get the job I want by:
<ul><li>relevant qualifications and expertise</li><li>key interpersonal skills</li><li>high energy</li><li>a record of quality results</li><li>initiative</li></ul>	<ul><li>anticipating questions</li><li>getting to know the organization</li><li>being prepared mentally and physically</li><li>creating a positive impression from the start</li><li>having something to say</li><li>feeling confident</li></ul>

It is vitally important that the interviewer selects the right person the first time round. Otherwise, they run the risk of upsetting the balance of the team with the wrong mix of skills, knowledge or experience or, at worst, have to suffer the expense in terms of time and cost of re-advertising and recruiting anew. Interviewers are also aware that the interview process itself is flawed, so the process is often made up of different steps.

First steps

Good interviewers will have invested a significant amount of time in the planning process – scoping the role, allocating a budget, talking to the stakeholders, defining the competencies and the person specification, planning the advertisement and briefing headhunters or recruitment consultants. After receiving applications, the tasks are far from over. The interviewer, or someone else in the organization, has to arrange the first steps:

1 Long-listing
2 Shortlisting
3 First interviews – sometimes on the telephone
4 Second interviews
5 Assessments
6 Meeting the stakeholders

Be aware that the more responsible the role, the more involved the key stakeholders will be. This may mean greater demands on your time because it may involve a series of meetings.

Telephone screening

The route to receiving an invitation to an interview can differ from organization to organization. Letters of application accompanied by CVs are the preferred way to present yourself and give information on your qualifications, experience and career to date. Increasingly, this information is presented online. Your aim is to sell yourself succinctly in no more than two pages, giving the reader what they need to make their decision. Some organizations use application forms, and the same applies to an application form as applies to a CV. Don't forget to sell yourself, even though your style may be cramped by the space available or questions asked – be creative.

Many organizations screen their long list of applicants by using a telephone interview. The purpose of the conversation is to create a realistic shortlist for the next stage. Only a small number of the candidates will progress beyond this stage, so don't underestimate the importance of this conversation.

Preparing for a telephone interview

A screening interview may be unannounced: don't be put off by this. The interviewer normally asks whether it is convenient to talk so you can always buy some time and ring the person back. If you are being interviewed by more than one person, be sure that you understand how to access the conference call and make sure that you are in an environment that is suitable and that you are not disturbed. Your preparation is essential – you will need to think through what you say, how you say it and what you want the interviewer to remember. Also consider the limits of time; while we know of screening interviews that have lasted over an hour, it is more likely that you will have under 20 minutes. Check who exactly you are speaking to and don't make any assumptions.

Case history

One senior manager, screening applicants for a key post in her team, rang an applicant to discuss certain aspects of his CV. He was unable to talk immediately. When he rang back, he assumed he was speaking to an administrative assistant and was both sharp and dismissive. Once he realized he was talking to his potential boss, his manner changed. But it was too late and there was no way he was going through to the next stage.

Telephone screening is one of the most challenging stages because it is extremely difficult to make an impact with only your voice. When you listen to an interview on the radio or have a telephone conversation, you probably listen to only a small amount of the conversation. Think about who you listen to, and why. What is it about their conversation that holds your attention? It's then up to you to build these techniques into your conversation with the interviewer! Use pace and tone to punctuate what you are saying. Think about what makes a voice attractive to you. Relax your jaw and mouth by repeating the sounds 'me – you' a number of times to help. If nothing else, it will make you laugh, which in turn will relieve any tension.

What to say

● Decide which parts of your CV to highlight.
● Make it interesting.
● Relate what you say to the role.

How to say it

● Speak clearly.
● Use tone and pace.
● Be relaxed.
● Smile.
● Stand up if you can.

Some organizations use video conferencing for the initial screening and they ask you to attend an anonymous office with what looks like a computer screen. Don't be put off by the technology. Arrive early and become familiar with the surroundings. In global organizations, this is as commonplace as a telephone link.

Elements of the interview

Every organization wants to make the best decision. The amount of investment in terms of time and money (advertising, recruiters'/agency costs, etc.) can be immense. This, balanced with the fact that interviews are proven to be one of the least reliable methods of selection, means that you will probably experience more than just a traditional question and answer session. The word 'interview' can be used to include a multitude of experiences, perhaps at an assessment centre, including:

- presentations
- group exercises
- tests – psychometric and ability tests
- a prioritizing exercise, known as 'in-tray'
- on-the-job assessments.

All of these exercises are devised to give you an opportunity to shine rather than to trip you up. Find out which of them you are likely to encounter at your interview and develop a strategy for managing them. It is likely that you have previously had to make a presentation, respond to a case study, contribute to a group discussion or manage your in-tray. If these are nothing new for you, but merely set in a different environment, you can be prepared for the unexpected. Remember that you have plenty of knowledge and experience to manage it well.

What often happens when individuals are asked to prepare for a presentation is that it becomes the only thing they focus on and they produce a wonderfully slick presentation, but everything else suffers. Whatever you are informed of in advance, it is worth preparing yourself for more – and even contacting the named person to find out more about the process.

Tests fall into a number of categories and they may be:

- verbal
- numerical
- skill
- spatial
- personality.

Skilled assessors should only choose tests that have a relevance to the role. You may be asked to complete some tests online; others will take place in a controlled environment and be timed. If you haven't sat such tests before, there are books and people who can help you.

TIP *Most parts of the interview process have an equal weighting, so overlooking any part in your preparation will affect your overall performance.*

What makes a question tough?

The concept of a tough question is usually a matter of personal interpretation. Sometimes an interviewer will deliberately ask what they consider to be a tough question; on other occasions they may hit your Achilles' heel without intent.

You may already have a clear idea of your 'tricky' areas. If so, it is a good idea to think about them now instead of hoping they might be missed. Compile a table like the one below to help you.

What would a tough question be about?	Why?	How will I combat this?
Gaps in employment		
Industry/technical		
Knowledge		
Health problems		
Why I am leaving		

If the question is tough because it is a surprise, either in content or timing, take a deep breath and think about what you have been asked. You can't prepare for the content of a surprise question, but you can prepare a general response. Practise the skill of checking with the interviewer that you have understood what has just been asked without simply echoing their question. *'Let me be clear – you are asking me ... So you want to know how I would ...'* This is a useful technique if the question requires you to go to a level of explanation that feels uncomfortable to you. This buys you some thinking time, too. Watch politicians; they are expert at this technique.

Why do interviewers ask 'tough' questions? In many cases, they want to gain a deeper understanding in a particular area – either a greater insight of you or to check the extent of your knowledge and expertise. They may need to test your response to the types of pressure demanded by the job.

The way to answer tough questions is to be confident that, if you have done your preparation, you will have a reasonable answer somewhere in your repertoire. Go for that rather than struggling to find a 'perfect' answer; just like the 'perfect' question, they don't exist! While every question the interviewer asks has a purpose, it is unwise to answer until you know:

- the reason for the question
- the most appropriate answer
- how to reply positively.

Over the next few days, notice whether your automatic responses to any questions tend to be framed in positive or negative language. When you use negative words like 'trouble', 'problem' and 'disaster', you base your thinking in a negative framework. The interviewer will join you there and be in a negative place, too. If you use language in a positive vein, then you will feel more confident and you can then expect the interviewer to respond in a more friendly and co-operative manner. Use words like 'opportunity', 'challenge' and 'learning'. Consider the different impacts and choose to be more positive.

Before every interview, do your research well and find out as much as possible about the job and the organization, not only from the information you are given but also from the company's website and company reports. For more information on how to conduct this research, see the companion to this book, **Job Interviews in a Week.**

Summary

Today we have considered all the stages leading up to the interview and their part in the recruitment process. You need to place equal importance on each stage of the process and preparing carefully helps – this is as much about finding out what to expect and tackling the uncertainty as about knowing exactly how to respond. Here are some simple rules to help you:

- Stay calm.
- Listen to the question.
- Speak clearly and steadily.
- Tell the truth.
- Avoid talking too much.
- Make it relevant.

You need to understand the interviewer, and by simply listening and reflecting back the language and pace of the interviewer you can demonstrate this understanding. By thinking about the question and what the interviewer wants to find out, you'll be able to answer comprehensively, presenting yourself well and leaving the interviewer with no need to ask supplementary questions.

SUNDAY
MONDAY
TUESDAY
WEDNESDAY
THURSDAY
FRIDAY
SATURDAY

Fact-check (answers at the back)

Some of these questions have more than one correct answer.

1. What is your objective for the interview?
a) Create a positive impression ❏
b) Find out more about the organization ❏
c) Gain experience ❏
d) Get the job ❏

2. In preparing for interviews, what should you do?
a) Confirm the time and date ❏
b) Squeeze it into a busy day ❏
c) Check who will be interviewing you ❏
d) Confirm how the interviewers will contact you ❏

3. In a telephone interview, what should you do?
a) Use tone and pace ❏
b) Relax ❏
c) Be at your normal desk ❏
d) Stand up ❏

4. How should you treat recruiters' calls?
a) With respect; they may be useful ❏
b) As a waste of time ❏
c) As a necessary evil ❏
d) With interest, even if the role isn't for you ❏

5. Before an assessment, what should you do the most preparation for?
a) The interview ❏
b) The presentation ❏
c) The group exercise ❏
d) All the component parts ❏

6. How would you identify a tough question?
a) As one that relates to your 'tricky' areas ❏
b) All questions are tough ❏
c) By seeing what you are asked on the day ❏
d) One on your current work ❏

7. How can you create thinking time?
a) By asking for clarification ❏
b) By writing the questions down ❏
c) By not responding immediately ❏
d) By giving a prepared answer ❏

8. Why do interviewers ask tough questions?
a) To trip you up ❏
b) To gain a deeper insight ❏
c) To check that your skills and experience match the role ❏
d) To see your response to pressure ❏

9. How should you respond to tough questions?
a) Think about the reason for the question ❏
b) With a model answer ❏
c) Positively ❏
d) Give the interviewer the answer you think they want ❏

10. Why should you research the organization/role?
a) To see whether it fits ❏
b) To pick up the language and style ❏
c) To show off at interview ❏
d) To prepare your questions ❏

MONDAY

Are you sitting comfortably?

You've passed the first stage of the recruitment process – well done! Your application and responses suggest that you could do the job and fit in. You've successfully answered the screening questions or passed the tests giving the recruiters the right information to aid the decision-making process. Your task now is to influence the interviewer to move from thinking that you 'could' do the job, to thinking you 'can' and 'will' do it successfully.

Whatever the next stage, it is important that you feel comfortable enough to succeed by:

- presenting yourself well
- meeting and greeting the interviewer(s) with ease
- establishing relationships
- making the right opening moves.

Presenting yourself well

If you have done your homework and prepared yourself well, you will be setting yourself up for success right from the start. Even before you meet the person who is going to interview you, you will be party to a mutual weighing up. It is often reported that interviewers make decisions within moments of meeting the interviewee and the remainder of the interview is spent building on that impression. Whatever your views on this, we would suggest that the opening stages of the interview are very influential, as both you and the interviewer want to impress each other.

The interviewer's objectives	The interviewee's objectives
To answer yes to these questions:	To answer yes to these questions:
● Did the interviewee impress all the people they met?	● Do I create a good impression?
● Could they do the job?	● Can I do myself justice?
● Do they look the part?	● Does the place feel and look good?
● Will they settle in quickly?	● Did they make me feel 'at home'?

SO PLEASED TO MEET YOU

The letter arrives or you receive a call inviting you to the interview. The first thing that comes into your head is normally a good indicator of how you feel about interviews – some people love the opportunity to talk about themselves; the thought of the experience is positive and the outcome excites them.

Other people dread interviews, often for one or more of the following reasons:

- they hate the predictability of the questions they will be asked
- they feel more competent than most of the interviewers they are faced with
- they don't like having to sell themselves
- they believe their experience and achievements should speak for themselves.

Positive thinking	Negative thinking
My application must have made an impression ...	Oh no! Do I really want the job ...?
I've got through the first stage ...	Can I be bothered to go through this routine again ...?
I'm obviously what they're looking for ...	What will I face ...? What exactly will they be looking for ...?
All I need to do is impress the interviewer ...	Can I do the job ...?

You should begin by thinking positively. If you are a person who tends to dread the interview process, your personal preparation should start immediately. If you have to ring to confirm your appointment, make sure that you have some prompts, which may include what you want to clarify. This may include these questions:

- Who will be interviewing me?
- What form will the interview take?
- Is there anything I should prepare before the interview?

Whatever your questions when contacting the organization, take a deep breath and start by smiling. Don't let your voice give away how you feel about the process.

You may have been told that you will be attending an informal interview. Beware: there is no such thing as an informal interview, and every meeting should be treated with careful thought, consideration and preparation.

Arriving

You will have checked the date, time and place of the interview and have arrived with time to spare. You should use this time to take in the surroundings. Relax, stand tall, breathe deeply and remember how you want to present yourself.

Entering the building

When you enter the building, take the opportunity to chat to the receptionist. Be natural, but don't present yourself as trying too hard to make a good impression, although it is one of your aims. The opinions of people at security and in reception, in fact any staff you might encounter, are often considered during the interview process.

> ## Case history
>
> 'Generally, my receptionist will see candidates first. I look carefully at their reaction to her – whether they treat her with respect and friendliness or disdain and condescension. I always ask her what she thinks overall and how she thinks the interviewee would fit into our department. It all affects my decisions.'

This cuts both ways. You will also have intuitive responses to the first people you meet, so attend to those responses.

Would you want to be represented by such people and could you work in those conditions? The overall efficiency and genuine customer service with which you are treated may impress you. On the other hand, you may be disappointed by being kept waiting or by the lack of organization – but also remember, it may be a bad day rather than an indicator of their style.

Remember that, for whoever you deal with from the start, you will be just one of their tasks for the day. As far as you are concerned, of course, you are the only person going for the interview.

How you present yourself counts. Make good eye contact, look around you and take notice of what you see and hear. These all give you a feel for the organization. There may be company literature to read, which can give you further insight, or even the basis for a question in the interview. They may offer you a drink, and it's fine to accept this, but you may have other things to do, such as:

- visiting the toilet
- checking your appearance
- reading your answers to questions
- preparing your responses
- relaxing.

Making a good first impression

First impressions are important, so how you sit, how you make eye contact with whoever approaches you, the quality of your handshake and how you look will all make an impact. Interviewers will notice unpolished shoes, dirty fingernails, an unironed shirt and quirky mannerisms. For most jobs, the impressions we make on our colleagues, clients and managers matter. How you look at the interview will be taken to indicate how you would look and conduct yourself when working.

You can anticipate their first words and prepare your responses accordingly. That way, you can avoid blurting out something nonsensical such as 'Goodnight' or 'Sorry'. If you know that you suffer from either verbal diarrhoea or paralysis when you're nervous, a few practised responses will stand you in good stead. Only continue your conversation with the receptionist or secretary if you get a favourable response. If the reception is busy, then the replies will be limited and you need to show your awareness of this.

Your first challenge is to introduce yourself and make polite and interesting conversation before you even start the interview. The earlier you can say your name, the better. It's something you know very well and because you don't have to think about it, you will be able to start with your 'normal' voice rather than a nervous, high-pitched squeak.

Your first words to whoever greets you first might include the following:

- 'Hello, I'm ... I've come for an interview with ...'
- 'What a fascinating building. How long have you been based here?'
- 'How does it compare with your offices at ...?'
- 'How do most people travel into work?'
- 'Do you have any company brochures I can read while I'm waiting?'

TIP *Make sure that you have thought about your opening remarks in advance. If you have a number of comments ready at the beginning, their familiarity will calm you down.*

Meeting and greeting with ease

When you enter the room, the interview is ready to begin – well, nearly. Sitting down and getting comfortable are important. It is likely that the room has been set out for an interview, but sometimes the interviewer will sit behind a desk. If you are not directed to a chair, it is appropriate to say, when invited to sit down: *Will this be OK?*

Be careful not to sit in direct sunlight, otherwise your squint or frown caused by the bright light may be misinterpreted as your normal expression. You may be asked if you want a drink. Do remember that juggling with a drink when you are talking may be difficult. Asking for water is the safest option, particularly as you can expect to be doing most of the talking.

If there is more than one interviewer, you should, at this stage, be introduced to all of them. A simple: *Yes, we've spoken*, or *Pleased to meet you*, gives you the chance to talk and keep your voice loosened. The interviewer may then describe the interview process, where this stage fits and what comes next. They may also describe the role you've applied for in the context of the organization. You may be asked at the end of this section whether everything is clear. A brief *Yes, thanks*, is all that's needed to signal that you're both ready to start. If you're unclear, ask for clarification.

The interviewer may then go through some of the same questions you have already been asked, so you will be well practised at answering these: 'How was your journey? Did you find us ok?' These questions are simply breaking the ice, so be careful not to go into a long monologue about transport, and resist the temptation to say the obvious or be sarcastic. This is not an opportunity to talk about the amount of traffic on the roads, how you hate commuting or the state of the public transport system. Your answers should be short but warm. If any conversation is to develop from this, make it positive. *Fine. The roads were clear and your map was a great help. I enjoy my travel time as it gives me time to plan.*

How long did it take you?

If this is the office base you will be working from, they will be interested in your commute. Research shows that because of the uncertainty surrounding employment, more people are establishing a home base and travelling to wherever their work is.

Most organizations, however, prefer that their employees live within a certain radius of their place of work and some even stipulate it. This question, while simple on the surface, may have an underlying query about your flexibility: *The train only took 35 minutes and I took advantage of that time.*

Establishing relationships

At this point, your intention is to relax and keep your voice active and loosened up. As well as settling yourself down, you want to get into the rhythm of the person with whom you are speaking. Research suggests that people tend to like people who are like them. If you make the effort to be like someone else, they will feel more comfortable in their dealings with you. (On Friday, we will consider how this relates to the question, 'Will you fit?')

Notice the pace at which the interviewer speaks, and try to speed up or slow down to match. Once you are synchronized, you may be able to lead them to a pace that better suits you.

Opening moves

What follows are a range of questions to warm you up, get you talking, giving both of you time to settle into the interview. Some of the toughest questions are those that give you enormous scope, such as:

- Talk me through your career to date.
- What are the highlights of your career?
- Take me through your CV/résumé/application form.
- What aspects of your career are particularly relevant to this role?

Most readers will have experienced questions such as these. They are used early in the interview to see how you cope and whether you are able to give a lucid and relevant response. Your interviewer wants to know how you present yourself in relation to your career. Your answer to these questions should give them clues to your suitability and the areas they may want to expand on later.

Don't panic when you hear these questions. You should be well prepared, in control and able to respond effectively. In preparing for the interview, you will have thought about your personality and strengths, picking out the qualities that show you are well matched to the organization and job, thus allowing you to describe how you are the ideal candidate.

You may choose to ask them: *Is there a particular part of my background that interests you?* Be aware of questions in response to questions, as they often do not give you the answers you want. They may respond with: 'The parts that equip you for this role!' The question: *Would you prefer a chronological or skills-based review?* may elicit the response: 'Whichever will give us the best overview of you.'

One other cautionary note is that this is a warm-up question; it is not intended to take the whole of the interview. Do not focus on every role, project and conversation you have had. The interviewer is still settling down and giving you something you can easily talk about to get the interview going.

Choose what you say carefully – your description of your career should be entertaining and no longer than one minute. You may decide to start by saying:

I see the start of my career as when I had to make choices at school and university as these have influenced all my future experiences.

I was clear what I wanted to do from an early stage and have followed that through a, b, c, while developing my skills ..., to the point that I reach today. I am now seeking an opportunity to stretch and develop myself further.

There are two significant themes in my career – my skills and the environments in which I have worked. I have developed my skills which are ... and my success has depended on them. The environments in which I have applied them are diverse ... I enjoy working in different environments.

SUNDAY
MONDAY
TUESDAY
WEDNESDAY
THURSDAY
FRIDAY
SATURDAY

I started my career at ... as I was seeking to ... I then sought to develop both my skills and knowledge by moving companies and chose to join ... because of their reputation for ... This has been the pattern throughout my career.

Whatever you say, you should demonstrate or refer to one or more of your key behavioural attributes. Your interviewers will want to know what you have done in addition to how you have done it. It will help them if you can look back to describe past achievements and then project forward to say how they will apply to and benefit this post.

You may, depending on the context, want to refer to:

- improvements
- turnover
- people managed
- projects completed
- savings instigated
- budgets managed.

This is a time for you to shine, so don't discuss problems you had with previous employers or managers. Take some time to think about yourself. These questions are not easy to answer off the cuff, but you can prepare for them.

Once you have safely navigated your way around these early questions, you can be confident and ready to concentrate on the more weighty ones that will undoubtedly follow.

Summary

You can be fully prepared for the questions you are likely to be asked at this early stage of the interview. We have reminded you of the most common opening questions, which are designed to help you both feel comfortable. Treat them as such and create answers that will allow your personality to shine through immediately you take your seat.

Decide in advance how you will answer the more generic warm-up questions, focusing on the parts of your career that are relevant to the role or the organization. Also have fixed in your mind the impression you want to create, how you want to be remembered by the interviewer. The early stages are also important for you to start to relax into the interview – so use them to your advantage.

Remember that, in the opening stages:

● everyone you meet may be asked for their opinion of you.
● there is no such thing as an informal interview.
● you can use your warm-up questions to your advantage.

SUNDAY

MONDAY

TUESDAY

WEDNESDAY

THURSDAY

FRIDAY

SATURDAY

Fact-check (answers at the back)

Some of these questions have more than one correct answer.

1. What should your reaction be to being invited to interview?
   a) You are excited at the prospect of a new role ❏
   b) You start to worry ❏
   c) You think about whether you want the job ❏
   d) You don't need to prepare ❏

2. Before you set off for interview, what should you check?
   a) The location ❏
   b) Date and time ❏
   c) How to get into the site ❏
   d) Who is interviewing you ❏

3. How should you judge the organization?
   a) By the interview starting on time ❏
   b) By how well you are treated ❏
   c) By whether you are offered a drink ❏
   d) By the quality of the facilities ❏

4. At interview, what should you pay attention to?
   a) Making eye contact ❏
   b) Your appearance ❏
   c) The room you are in ❏
   d) Your hands ❏

5. What should your first words to the person who greets you be?
   a) What should I know about the person interviewing me? ❏
   b) Do you enjoy working here? ❏
   c) What's the money like? ❏
   d) Hello I'm ... and I'm here for ... ❏

6. When asked if you'd like a drink, how should you respond?
   a) Water would be great ❏
   b) A gin and tonic ❏
   c) Only if you are having one ❏
   d) Do you have soya milk? ❏

7. In the opening stages of the interview, what should you try to do?
   a) Create a good impression ❏
   b) Impress the interviewer ❏
   c) Assess the organization ❏
   d) Make the interviewer laugh ❏

8. If asked about your journey, how should you respond?
   a) The roads were clear ❏
   b) The map was a great help ❏
   c) It was a nightmare, public transport! ❏
   d) Your postcode didn't work on my satnav ❏

9. What should you do when you talk about your career?
   a) Go into details of roles ❏
   b) Focus on achievements ❏
   c) Say it's difficult to summarize ❏
   d) Ask how far back they'd like you to go ❏

10. In describing your career, what should you focus on?
    a) Achievements ❏
    b) Problems ❏
    c) The culture of the organization ❏
    d) Your relationship with your boss ❏

TUESDAY

Can you do the job?

The introductions are over. You are in the interview room. Your interviewer has talked you through the role, the organization and the format of the interview. You sense that the interview for real is about to begin. At this stage of the interview, the interviewer has certain objectives; he or she believes you have the experience to do the job from your application, but this stage is about really convincing him or her that you 'can' do the job and make a contribution to the organization.

Today we will focus on the following areas:

- Work history and experience
- Training and qualifications
- Competence

Normally, this phase of the interview is not populated by the toughest questions. The interviewer is wanting factual answers, but don't waste an opportunity – tell your interviewers not just what you have done in the past, but what led to your success, the difference you made, what this has taught you for the future and how this relates to the role you are applying for. Don't waste any opportunity to sell yourself and the benefits you could bring to the role, team or organization.

Your work history and experience

Your jobs, projects, experience, achievements and career choices are of interest to the interviewer at this stage.

Do you have what they need to do the job? They will ask:

- What have you done?
- What have you achieved?
- In what ways have you achieved your goals?
- Why do you want to leave your current job?

I GOT A LOT OUT OF THAT JOB AND NEXT...

The interviewer's objectives	The interviewee's objectives
To have positive answers to these questions:	To demonstrate that:
	● I could do the job, given the opportunity
● Can you do the job?	● I have the skills and experience you need
● Do you have the skills and experience?	● I am articulate
● Do you match your CV?	● My achievements speak for themselves
● Are you qualified?	● I could add value
● Do you match our competencies?	

What have you done?

Your response to questions in this section should recognize the interviewer's motivation for asking them. They are not wanting a regurgitation of your job titles or organizations; they want to go below the surface to hear about how you have contributed to the success of the team, department, organization or group. Their questions may reflect this, but even if they don't, your answers should!

Talk me through your career to date.

This question is asked for a variety of reasons. As we mentioned yesterday, it can be used as a warm-up, or it can be used to reacquaint them with your CV. Your interviewer should already have read through your CV so in this question they want a 'whistle-stop' tour of what you've done.

We emphasize the whistle-stop, so be succinct and precise! Make sure that your words match what you have put on paper, and beware of too much detail such as dates, who you reported to, responsibilities.

My career has spanned four different organizations and has been about acquiring knowledge and skills and applying these to each different role. Each role has contributed to the person I am today and supports the contribution I can make to your company.

What brings you here?

Your interviewer may ask this question in a variety of different ways. This question indicates that your interviewer is interested in the choices you have made in your career, and how your skills have developed through your different roles and organizations. You have to be selective in your answers and choose the elements that demonstrate individual and organization benefits.

I have enjoyed a successful and varied career. My first job gave me an opportunity to develop my people management and leadership skills. I managed a team of 40 on three different sites, establishing set procedures and monitoring service levels. I then moved on to develop more specialist skills in a sister organization, managing projects and achieving this within the timescales set, always coming in under budget and on target. I am now seeking an opportunity in which I can bring together both these sets of skills and develop them.

Tell me about your responsibilities in your present job.

This is not an opportunity to recite the 20 responsibilities outlined in your job description or your competencies. It's an opportunity to blow your own trumpet. Wherever possible, summarize your responsibilities. The more you can describe them in terms of the benefits they bring to the organization, the better.

I have four main responsibilities ... Balancing these and setting targets to ensure that my team achieves them has been a challenge, particularly in a climate of managing a reduced cost base. I have been successful and my success in the role has been due to my ability to manage and control the work of the team.

What have you achieved?

This style of question is relatively easy to respond to, if you have prepared.

How is your effectiveness in your present post measured?

Measures are important to most organizations. Even if your role isn't formally measured, you should think about how you quantify your success. It gives the interviewer some ideas of the scope of your role, what you have achieved and the potential contribution you could make to their organization.

The principal measure is the business review process. I have both a cost and a revenue budget for which I am fully accountable. The bottom line is what counts most. Apart from this, I have the freedom to make decisions. I enjoy being measured as I can always focus my attention on identifying and working towards improvements.

Tell me about a recent project. What aspects of it gave you the most satisfaction?

Pick a good example. Don't just go for personal satisfaction, although that is the essence of the question. Also focus on the immediate – and long-term – benefits.

They asked me to reorganize a department. I did my research, reading and talking to the key stakeholders. I identified four key improvements that could save over £50,000 a year and implemented them over the next two months.

Have you done the best work you are capable of?

Say 'yes' and the interviewer will think you're a 'has been'. Your focus on this question should be on how you could apply and develop your skills further.

I'm proud of my work achievements to date. But I believe the best is yet to come. I'm always motivated to give my best efforts and in this job there are always opportunities to contribute and improve.

In what ways has your job prepared you to take on greater responsibility?

The interviewer is looking for examples of professional development, perhaps to judge your future growth potential, so you must tell a story that demonstrates this.

When I first started, my boss would brief me daily. I made mistakes, learned a lot and met all my deadlines. As time went by I took on greater responsibilities. Now I meet with her weekly to discuss any strategic changes so that she can keep the senior team informed. I think that demonstrates not only my growth but also the confidence my manager has in my judgement and ability to perform consistently above standard.

In what ways have you achieved your goals?

What has made you successful in your current position?

Here, the interviewer is trying to find out not just what, but how. You may want to talk about your influencing skills, your persistence, your understanding of the business needs, timing or whatever else has made you successful.

I believe my success is due to my ability to recognize who it is I need to get on my side. I then start to influence them by identifying the business benefits and getting them to sponsor the project at the highest level. I keep these people constantly updated on progress, giving them an opportunity to continue to contribute by challenging the blocks I experience.

What problems have you met in relationships with your present colleagues and what techniques have you developed to overcome them?

We only achieve things in organizations through other people, but often we do experience blocks of some kind. This doesn't mean that the interviewer expects problems with the role or your relationships; it means that they are trying to uncover what strategies you have for dealing with disappointments, blocks, obstacles or the culture of the organization in which you have worked. You should be honest and positive about how you have tackled these; you may want to include a bit about your learning.

My role was about change and I knew there would be resistance. The resistance I experienced was subtle – it involved only giving me a part of the story, not following through on actions and undermining me with colleagues. The best technique I found for dealing with this was by recording on paper all key conversations where decisions were made, giving timescales for action. I would then distribute them to all the other key stakeholders. It seemed to work. My colleagues understood that I would not lie down and accept their behaviour and they changed. This isn't my preferred style but I adapted my style to the people and the situation.

What are the most difficult decisions you have made in the last six months? What made them difficult?

Your interviewer is interested in what you find difficult and wherever possible you should balance this with a strength. You may want to talk about managing people, or others' expectations or that you have stretch goals and this challenges you in terms of prioritizing.

Due to the cost of savings that had to be achieved, I needed to make a member of my team redundant. It was a very tough decision as she made a valuable contribution to the team, but I just needed to find a more cost-effective way to deliver. My biggest challenge was to communicate this to her in a way she understood and was not too damaging. I think I achieved this through careful planning and preparation.

How do you feel about your progress to date?

This question is not only about your progress but also asks you to rate your self-esteem. Be positive. Help the interviewer believe that you see each day as an opportunity to learn and contribute; that you see their organization's environment being conducive to your best efforts.

In looking back over my career I am very pleased about my progress. I have achieved all that I have set myself and more. I have identified opportunities that would stretch and develop me and been pleased with my achievements. I am now seeking to maintain this momentum.

Why do you want to leave your current job?

Questions on the decisions you made that prompted you to seek a change in your role or organization should be answered with a degree of caution. Many people, when answering these questions, fall into the trap of focusing on what isn't right rather than what is. Focus on the 'pulls' (what drove you forward) rather than the 'pushes' (what made you want to leave).

Pull factors	Push factors
Seeking fresh challenge	Boredom
New organization/products	Relationship with boss
Working with new people	Asked to resign
Belief in vision	Redundancy

ADMIN   R+D

What made you want to leave – after ten years with them?

Here the underlying question is 'What went wrong?'

Organizations are now looking for a mixture of loyalty and exposure to different environments, cultures, projects and people. In answering this question, you have to walk the fine line between demonstrating this loyalty and commitment while seeking fresh challenges and being flexible and adaptable. Make sure that you also place whatever moves you have made within a context of a long-term strategy, even if it didn't feel like that at the time – every move should be seen as moving towards a career goal.

I wanted a position that would give me more responsibility, a position in which I could put into practice what I had been learning. I recognized that this wasn't available to me at ...

What do you want from your next job that isn't in your current position?

This question has a slight twist in its tail. It should always be answered positively and be tailored to the position you are applying for.

An opportunity to apply my ... skills in a new team, with a different set of customers and in a different environment. The challenge will come from all those changes. I know I can make a contribution and from what you've been describing, it sounds even more exciting.

Why have you applied for this job?

This is one question you should expect. It it doesn't come in this form, it may be couched in *why* ...(the organization)?

You need to be sure of 'why' as it will be obvious from your body language if you are not convinced, committed or clear. Your reasons may be opportunity, challenge and association.

From all I know about the role, it is exactly what I am looking for. My knowledge of your organization, from talking to employees and reading the literature, tells me that this is somewhere I would fit in particularly well and I know I can make a contribution.

Your training and qualifications

Interviewers tend not to make assumptions on the basis of people's qualifications because they are more interested in people's competence. Competence relates to the skills, knowledge and behaviours which, combined, produce the required results. This generally reflects a shift from the concept of education to the concept of learning: from input (classroom-based learning) to outputs (self-paced learning, coaching); from becoming qualified to being fully developed. You will probably be asked less about the institutions or courses you've attended, and more about how you have applied your learning.

What have you done since you first qualified to keep your knowledge up to date?

The interviewer is keen to understand how you are developing in the context of your practices and the changes in the external environment. You can demonstrate this in a range of ways – books, coaching, shadowing, conferences, project groups, reviews, training courses, professional associations, journals, the Internet. Make sure that you give a balanced response. Present yourself as someone who has taken responsibility for their own development and seeks regular opportunities to learn.

I read journals and papers. I attend workshops through my professional institute. I seek opportunities to shadow those I feel I can learn from and attend courses and conferences.

Which of your qualifications do you see as relevant to this post, and how?

In answering this question you need to think carefully about what skills this role requires. If it's a technical role, then you should refer to your technical qualifications and experience. If it's more a management role, then refer to whatever training or qualifications you have. Do not be put off if you don't have formal qualifications. Talk through your learning.

My degree, while some time ago, has given me a good grounding in the principles, models and practice of ... While I have studied for my Masters and a Diploma in Management Studies, the qualifications most relevant to the role are not so much of the accredited type, but more to do with 10 years of success in the role with both personal and professional achievements.

What important changes are taking place in your field? Do you consider them to be good or bad?

This question tests how up to date you are, so you may want to clarify it in terms of your function or sector. They are also asking for your opinion, which is a little more tricky; all you can do is be honest. Your interviewer is not wanting someone who sits on the fence, but if there are good and bad points you should state them. Think about what 'good' and 'bad' means to you, and what they might mean to the interviewer. The role or organization may give you some indicators here – so that in a technology company, technology provides opportunity rather than threat.

We think you might be over-qualified for this job!

If you were over-qualified for the job, would you be applying for it? In an interviewer's mind, it could be that you are desperate. A future employer doesn't want to think that they are going to take you on and you are going to be bored within weeks, or that you are seeing this as a stepping stone to another opportunity. You should respond that everything you do you do to the best of your ability and you still feel you have a lot to learn.

Your competence

As we mentioned previously, competencies are now commonplace in most organizations. They don't simply focus on *what* you do, but *how* you do it.

Competencies make the interview process much more focused and less dependent on the intuition and gut reaction of the interviewer. The competencies needed for the role are normally available to applicants. If you haven't received a list of these, then do request them as they are an essential part of your preparation. By reading them, you will get an idea of the culture and what is important to the organization. You can then frame your answers to reflect this.

Competencies may also include characteristics such as resilience and influence. The questions you may be asked in order to uncover these areas of competence may be:

Resilience

● How do you bounce back after a setback?
● How would I know you were under pressure?
● In what ways has your boss disappointed you?
● What does resilience mean to you?
● When have you demonstrated resilience?

Relate your answers to your own experience and related aspects of your work, not how you recovered after having a puncture on the way to an airport.

Influencing

● Describe a time when you got the solution you wanted.
● Whose support have you found elusive, and why?

- How do you influence others?
- Tell me when you persuaded someone senior to do something they were unwilling to do.
- I have a preferred candidate for this role – change my mind.
- Which areas of influence challenge you most?

> **TIP** *These questions offer you an opportunity to sell yourself to the interviewer. Be focused and clear, and come across as just the person they need to make a meaningful contribution to their organization.*

Summary

Today we have concentrated on the questions concerned with: *Can you do the job?* This is a straightforward part of the interview in so far as the interviewers are building up a picture of how you present what you have achieved to date. They want to hear your approach to describing your 'history'. It's an opportunity for you to relax into the interview and form a relationship with the interviewer ready for next stages.

While this part of the interview is straightforward, it is possible not to perform at your best and to avoid this we'd suggest you think about your career to date and how to bring what you've done to life:

- Sell yourself.
- Make sure that your words complement what you have said on paper.
- Present your career in a logical, planned and progressive manner.
- Convince the interviewer that you 'can do the job'.
- Present your learning in terms of competence, not solely formal qualifications.
- Refer to transferable skills.

Fact-check (answers at the back)

Some of these questions have more than one correct answer.

1. How should you demonstrate you can do the job?
   a) By referring to skills ❏
   b) By talking about your experience ❏
   c) By demonstrating that you could add value ❏
   d) By focusing on qualifications ❏

2. In describing your career to date, what should you do?
   a) Talk about your roles ❏
   b) Read from your CV ❏
   c) Highlight how you've contributed to success ❏
   d) Focus on the details of your responsibilities ❏

3. The question about what brings you here relates to what?
   a) How you travelled to the interview ❏
   b) Choices you've made ❏
   c) How your skills developed ❏
   d) What you've experienced ❏

4. By what can your effectiveness in your role be measured?
   a) Detailed descriptions of your key performance indicators ❏
   b) Your contribution to the social club ❏
   c) How many people you managed ❏
   d) Your contribution to the organization ❏

5. When talking about what gives you satisfaction, what should you do?
   a) Focus on your likes ❏
   b) Describe the things you dislike ❏
   c) Pick a good example ❏
   d) Talk about what other people say about you ❏

6. To answer the question about responsibility, what should you do?
   a) Refer to your CV ❏
   b) Talk about being ready for more responsibility ❏
   c) Demonstrate how you have taken on more responsibilities ❏
   d) Describe the limits of your current role ❏

7. When talking about problems, what should you do?
   a) Describe difficult people ❏
   b) Ask the interviewer why they are asking the question ❏
   c) Focus on problems ❏
   d) Describe how you overcame problems ❏

8. When describing difficult decisions, what should you do?
   a) Talk honestly about what you find difficult ❏
   b) Describe a difficult manager ❏
   c) Focus on feedback you've received ❏
   d) Describe a number of difficult decisions ❏

9. What are questions relating to competencies focusing on?
a) Whether you are competent ❏
b) Why you do things a certain way ❏
c) Skills, knowledge and behaviours ❏
d) How you do things ❏

10. What are the reasons for questions on why you left roles?
a) Why you are leaving ❏
b) What attracts you to the new role ❏
c) Whether you'd fit in ❏
d) Whether you'd stay ❏

SUNDAY

MONDAY

TUESDAY

WEDNESDAY

THURSDAY

FRIDAY

SATURDAY

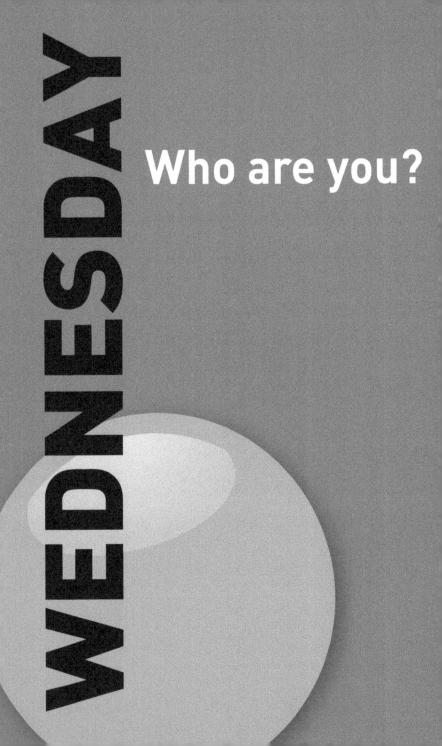

WEDNESDAY

Who are you?

So far this week, we've been focusing on what you have done in your career, and you should now be able to talk confidently and convincingly about your experience, skills, competence and qualifications.

Today considers questions relating to who you are. We will look at how you can convey who you are and what you can bring to the role in terms of:

- self-assessment
- personality
- achievements
- strengths and weaknesses
- other people's perceptions
- leisure.

Interviewers want you to bring to life the person you presented in your CV or application, and their questions will now relate to 'how' you will do the job rather than what you will do. Depending on the type of job, they will need to know whether you are a team player or a loner, a creative or a project manager. They will be constantly asking themselves whether you are the kind of person they need for the post.

The interviewer's objectives	The interviewee's objectives
To have positive answers to these questions:	To be able to:
● Does your personality fit?	● describe myself succinctly
● Are you easy to get to know?	● portray my personality accurately
● Can you talk about yourself?	● be honest and open

We would encourage you to give an assessment of yourself which shows a confident and informed individual. Be intuitive: put yourself in the interviewer's shoes. You want the interviewer to feel that you can get along with them, your team and other stakeholders, all in the context of their organization. This is your opportunity to make the most of yourself. The skill is to get the balance right. There is a fine line between confidence and over-confidence, between your achievements and what you've achieved through your team, between targets you've set and challenges that were set by the organization.

> **TIP** Spend time thinking about the way you talk about yourself and your work – your team's and your organization's achievements, your work and leisure – and give the interviewer a rounded impression of you the person.

Self-assessment

Self-knowledge is increasingly important in the world of work. You are expected to know yourself – your skills, characteristics and limitations. You are expected to understand what impact these may have on your performance and, of course, be seeking to develop and improve. The interviewer will be interested in how you manage self-assessment questions. For your part, you need to think about the *you* you want to present. Some people find all the questions that ask them to describe themselves *tough*. If this is you, it is well worth spending some time analysing your anxiety and working out ways to combat it. The key to overcoming anxiety is planning and practice, so think about your responses in advance and practise saying them out loud.

Anxiety	Solution
Once I start talking, I won't know when to stop.	Write the main points and time yourself as you say them – aim for no more than 2 minutes.
I've nothing to say about myself.	Complete the sentence 'I am . . .' at least 50 times and then assess your responses.
How can I know what they want?	Go back to your earlier research and note the type of person you would be looking for to fill the post. Pick out what relates to you.
They will think I'm arrogant.	They want you to be confident about yourself and aware of who you are. Select truthful evidence.

It is certain that these kinds of questions will emerge at some stage during the interview, so overcome your anxiety if it exists. Be proud of who you are, and what you have achieved, and present it in a way that convinces the interviewer. Use every source of information to inform your preparation. Ask colleagues for feedback, look over the comments from your appraisals, think about projects you were particularly proud of or enjoyed. If you have completed tests, these may help. All these sources say something about who you are. Also think about examples to back up statements, as your interviewers will be interested in how you present the evidence. Self-assessment questions come in a variety of forms, the most common of which are:

- Tell me about yourself.
- How would you describe yourself?
- What are you like as a person?
- How would your colleagues describe you?

It is worth experimenting with different statements to describe who you are. Take a couple of sentences from your 'I am' list and play around with them: *I am an ideas person ... I am easy going ... I am in charge of ... I enjoy challenges ...*

Now start to flesh out your statements with examples that demonstrate how they relate to the job and the organization. Create a sense of your value to the potential employer and the benefits you can offer. Prepare a statement that is powerful, accurate and that demonstrates what differentiates you from other candidates:

> *I am creative and identify unconventional ways of tackling a situation. At ..., I had a reputation for making suggestions that saved the company time and money, while preserving the company image.*

Answers to these questions will flow with practice. The skill is to make them relevant to your role and your interviewer.

Personality

You may be asked some questions that relate to specific personality types and traits that are considered necessary for the post. For example, if you are applying to manage a remote location, you will need to have a degree of independence; for a customer relations post, you will need to demonstrate tolerance and patience. Consider how the personality traits below apply to you and the jobs you want.

Personality traits

Independence – Making decisions without supervision or reference

Patience – Calm and prepared to wait for the right time and place

Integrity – Takes responsibility for own actions, good and poor

Judgement – Evaluates data and courses of action rationally

Adaptability – Responds effectively to change

Compliance – Adheres to company policy/procedures

Tenacity – Demonstrates staying power in challenging situations

Commitment – Belief in job/role and its value to the company

Decisive – Readiness to take actions and make decisions

Dependability – Staying power and stamina

Confidence – Calmly aware and comfortable with who you are

However you describe your personality, be sure to have substantive examples and, wherever possible, give times and benefits:

I pride myself on my ability to act on my own initiative. We were keen to take on a project to assess waste management. There was no spare money to do this, so I spoke to various local organizations to arrange a sponsorship programme.

Here are some other questions to think through.

What are your likes?

This is a rather vague question, but it may be chosen in contrast to what you are like as a person to see how you respond.

I like challenges. I always set personal goals to try and push myself that bit further and to feel I've achieved something.

What are your dislikes?

This inevitably follows 'What are your likes?'. The interviewer may be wanting to know how compatible your personal values are with the role.

Be wary of criticizing your former boss and colleagues, or implying that you were unhappy about working hard, doing boring tasks or dealing with the less pleasant aspects of your work. Also steer clear of launching into a tirade about dislikes of soaps, fast food and other trivia.

I try to be honest and act with integrity. I dislike it when others lie, blame or don't show the same commitment to the task or the company as I do.

How have you benefited from your disappointments?

Disappointments are different from failures. It is an intelligent interviewer who asks this question. The question itself is very positive – it enables you to talk about what you have learned from your setbacks and how it has changed your approach.

I treat disappointments as learning: I look at what has happened, why it happened and how I would do things differently at each stage should I face the same situation again.

Be yourself when you are answering these questions. After all, it's not just what you say; it's the way that you say it. Part of your personality will shine through as you utter your response. Notice whether your body language complements or refutes your descriptions. It is no good suggesting that patience is one of your qualities if your foot is tapping in anticipation of the next question or, when talking about your energy and enthusiasm, you talk into your chest with a sullen expression.

Strengths and limitations

It is well recognized that people have both strengths and limitations. There will be parts of your personality that support you and other parts that trip you up. Interviewers ask about strengths and limitations as another way of assessing your knowledge of yourself, your honesty and your objectivity. They may also talk about weaknesses, areas for improvement or personal development.

Before the interview, you should spend some time thinking about the characteristics that make you successful in everything you undertake. What has contributed to making you who you are today? It helps enormously if you can portray a sense of self-worth and confidence in what you do well. If you can excite the interviewer with your enthusiasm, they will assume you can do the same with their internal and external customers.

I pride myself on being able to build rapport quickly with new people. In fact, at ... I was often asked to take visitors around the plant because the MD knew I would make them feel welcome and important.

Think through examples of your strengths balanced against the expectations for the job. For example, a manager might be expected to have strengths in planning, delegating, budgeting, time management, influencing people and managing relationships.

The interviewer will also expect you to give examples of how you are working to improve your limitations. Think about what might have held you back in your career. What has led you to feel frustrated and unhappy at work? You may come across some familiar areas for development that you can usefully admit to in an interview. Do remember that limitations can simply be the reverse side of a strength:

My eye for detail can be a great strength in designing copy, but a limitation when I'm managing people, as I need to be convinced that everything is as it should be.

You have choices in presenting your limitations – you could focus on those strictly related to the post:

I am not familiar with the software you use. I became proficient with our present system in about three weeks and I'm sure I could do so with yours.

Or you can relate to your personality:

I am very particular about the way work goes out to clients. In my last appraisal, we discussed the way this sometimes slows down output. We also agreed that without such attention to detail our consistency and accuracy could be affected. I am working on finding a more balanced approach.

Some questions refer indirectly to strengths and limitations:

Tell me about the last time you didn't delegate work to a member of your team and you were left with too much to do. How did you feel about it? How did you handle the situation differently next time?

What are the most difficult situations you've faced?

How do you define 'difficult'? You must have a story ready for this one in which the situation was both tough and flexible enough to allow you to show yourself in a good light.

Avoid talking about matters to do with other people. You can talk about a difficult situation that resulted in a disciplinary, but emphasize that once you had examined the problem and reached a conclusion you acted quickly and professionally, with the best interests of the company at heart.

How well do you work in a stressful environment?

Most jobs have an element of stress, whether it's working to very tight deadlines or handling lots of different projects or priorities. Your answer to this question should encompass examples of when you have successfully navigated your way through stressful situations.

What do you not have that we need for this post?

This is an easy response:

I think my skills match your requirements. I need more detailed product knowledge and experience of the company procedure.

Achievements

Achievements should be easy to identify. There is always something in our careers or lives that we feel particularly proud of: a project completed on time and budget against all odds; a crisis averted; people you developed; a bid that you won; a person you influenced. In fact, it could be anything that had a positive outcome. You should judge the merits of sticking to job-related accomplishments or whether it is appropriate to expand into your life outside the workplace.

I was proud to be part of the team that successfully guided the company towards a quality award.

I raised £ ... for charity running in the London Marathon. I also picked up some business from my fellow runners along the way.

What has been your most creative achievement at work?

Although I feel my biggest achievements are still ahead of me, I am proud of my involvement in ... with ... I made my contribution as part of that team and learned a lot in the process. We succeeded through hard work, concentration and an eye for the bottom line.

What makes you stand out from the crowd?

A simple question, but it requires some thought. You can answer it in terms of increased revenues, decreased operational costs, streamlined work flow. You may also want to think in terms of your characteristics:

I have a great track record for assuming responsibilities above and beyond the call of duty and I'm always willing to go the extra mile to get the job done well.

This reveals focus, direction, a sense of strength and determination. There are many different styles of 'achievement' questions:

Tell me about some of the toughest groups that you have had to get co-operation from. Did you have any formal authority? What did you do?

Other people's perceptions

Once you have given an account of your ideas about yourself, you are likely to be asked what other people think of you. Take care not to be flippant or to regurgitate what you have already said. Also, be mindful that some of the people mentioned may have written, or be about to write, your references. It is important to be consistent. Ideally, it would be good to check with your referees what they might write. Where that is not possible, try to recall conversations and appraisal discussions you have had with them. You may be asked a selection of the following questions:

- How might your current colleagues describe you?
- What would your boss tell me about you?
- What is likely to be in your references?
- How would your team describe you?
- How might one of your closest friends describe you?
- How might your worst enemy describe your character?

In my last appraisal, my manager said how much he appreciated my candour. He knows that I think very carefully before giving feedback and then do so in a professional way.

My staff know that I represent them positively in any organizational issues that may concern them. I know from feedback at appraisals that they trust me to keep their interests at the top of my agenda.

Don't underestimate the power of other people's perceptions. Remember our comments from Monday that the perception people have of you will count. Anxiety can create the wrong impression, so by managing your anxiety you should be better able to manage perceptions.

Leisure

What you do in your leisure time is an important part of who you are. Because of the commitment that work now demands, interviewers are wanting to hear about the balance you strive for, to conserve your energy or simply to recuperate and switch off from the challenges of the day. It also gives the interviewer a fuller picture of who you are outside work. The following questions are a selection of those you may be asked:

- If you were on a desert island, what book would you take, and why?
- What was the last book you read/film you saw and how did it affect you?
- How do you relax?
- What do you do for your holidays?
- What do you do in the evenings and at weekends?

Be prepared for these questions. It makes sense to decide before the interview whether there is a particular film or book you want to mention because it says something about you that you want to convey.

Do you escape into thrillers and spy stories, or immerse yourself in science fiction? You may be a fan of the classics or poetry, romance, politics or sport.

Many people enjoy personal development books or tapes – there are no right or wrong answers, and these are not trick questions. Having said that, it is crucial that you have read or seen whatever you discuss so that you can talk about it with knowledge and enthusiasm.

Case history

We spoke to one candidate who, at interview, enthused about *Pride and Prejudice* and was asked if they had read *Middlemarch*. They replied honestly, 'no', and were relieved when the interviewer suggested that it was a book they thought the candidate would thoroughly enjoy. Imagine the embarrassment if they had said 'yes', and then been expected to discuss it.

How do you wind down after a busy and pressured time at work?

With increasing awareness of the long-term effects of stress, enlightened employers are recognizing the importance of recovery time for their staff. It is important to demonstrate that you know how to look after yourself and keep yourself mentally and physically agile.

I work away a lot and take care that I either go for a swim, a sauna or a walk to orientate myself and to get a break from the office environment.

Whatever you do or choose to refer to, make sure it involves doing something constructive and worthwhile.

Summary

Today we focused on all the dimensions that make you unique. The *who are you* questions provide you with the opportunity to blow your own trumpet and talk proudly about your achievements and successes. You should feel free to talk about your ambitions and ideas for the future.

It's good to collect comments that people make about you in both structured feedback such as appraisals and 360 feedback, but also in the course of a day or a week. You could also extend this to what customers say about the service you provide. Create a portfolio of statements that could fit into this part of the interview. Read through it regularly and think what it says about you. That way you will have material from which to select appropriately, whatever interview you attend.

- Prepare for questions about you the person.
- Identify what makes you different
  – your unique selling point.
- Think through your achievements.
- Research how other people perceive you.

SUNDAY

MONDAY

TUESDAY

WEDNESDAY

THURSDAY

FRIDAY

SATURDAY

Fact-check (answers at the back)

Some of these questions have more than one correct answer.

1. In assessing yourself, what are you expected to be able to describe?
a) Your skills ❏
b) The details of your sickness record ❏
c) Your characteristics ❏
d) How others see you ❏

2. When asked to describe yourself, what should you do?
a) Talk at length ❏
b) Have planned what you will say ❏
c) Say you prefer not to ❏
d) Change the subject ❏

3. In preparing for self-assessment questions, what should you do?
a) Look back through appraisals ❏
b) Think about your successes ❏
c) Ask your colleagues for feedback ❏
d) Refer to your psychometrics ❏

4. Which of these is an example of a personality trait?
a) Patience ❏
b) Office clown ❏
c) Tenacity ❏
d) Integrity ❏

5. When asked what others say about you, what should you do?
a) Make a joke ❏
b) Quote your referees ❏
c) Refer to your appraisals ❏
d) Mention 360 feedback ❏

6. How should you answer a question about your limitations?
a) Describe situations when things have gone wrong ❏
b) By changing the subject ❏
c) By describing your personality ❏
d) By saying how you are working to improve them ❏

7. In answering a question on disappointments, what should you focus on?
a) Learning ❏
b) What disappoints you in others ❏
c) How disappointed you have become with your current organization ❏
d) Setbacks ❏

8. When talking about yourself, what should your body language do?
a) Support what you are saying ❏
b) Undermine what you are saying ❏
c) Give the impression of supreme confidence ❏
d) Show signs of stress ❏

9. In talking about your achievements, what should you do?
a) Refer back to your education ❑
b) Talk about the academic achievement of your children ❑
c) Focus on your achievements at work ❑
d) Describe something that had a positive outcome ❑

10. In talking about your leisure time, what should you refer to?
a) Your many out-of-work activities ❑
b) The last book you read ❑
c) Your perfect weekend ❑
d) How you relax ❑

THURSDAY

How will you do the job?

Yesterday we concentrated on giving the interviewer an impression of *who you are*. We hope that you are now feeling more confident about describing yourself, the person, in ways that fully represent your achievements and successes as well as telling interviewers about your roles. Today we will take this a step further. It is not just you or your skills, experience and knowledge that the interviewer is interested in, but how these come together and *how you do the job*.

You may have experienced situations when you've planned something well – all the component parts are great – but when you mix them together, things go disastrously wrong. You may be a brilliant candidate, with all the essential and desirable characteristics and experience, but your interviewer may sense that your methods of working do not match those of your prospective line manager or department. As we discussed earlier in the week, where this is destructive, it can also be costly.

Today we will guide you through the relevant questions:

- Why this job?
- What is your management style?
- What motivates you?

Why this job?

Knowing how you will do the job you have applied for is essential to the interviewer and contributes to their view of your fit.

The interviewer's objectives	The interviewee's objectives
To get answers to these questions:	To demonstrate:
● What is your management style?	● my style, with examples
● What motivates you?	● what I want from work
● How do you motivate others?	● how I manage my team
● How does this fit with the culture?	● how I could add value
● What blocks might you experience?	● my fit and flexibility
● How does your style complement others?	● how my style complements others

Why do you want this job? is a predictable interview question. It may not be quite so direct, but at some point during the interview it will emerge. Consider the different ways of answering it.

Because it ...

● was advertised
● matches my skills
● is the right time to be moving
● appealed to me.

I was ...

● excited by the advertisement
● seeking a challenge
● planning my next move.

The 'because it' list has more of the 'push' factors that we mentioned on Tuesday; the 'I was' list contains more of the 'pull' factors. There is only a slight difference in the response, but if you choose your words carefully you will sound planned, focused and proactive.

This only becomes a tough question when you haven't thought through your response. Is it a question you have ever seriously asked yourself? This is a good opportunity to work out what makes a job appealing to you and what might lessen its attraction. We are suggesting three key areas for you to think about:

CURRENT JOB

PROSPECTIVE JOB

- identity
- values
- preferred environment.

Identity

We often frame our understanding of our identity around what we do, rather than who we are. This is why yesterday we took you through a step-by-step approach to understanding yourself. When you describe yourself to a stranger you may say: *I'm a team leader, a programmer, a manager.* Much of our status comes from our title. We like shorthand ways to describe ourselves but this only conveys a part of the picture – the 'what' rather than the 'how'. There is a huge difference between identifying yourself as a project manager or as the central co-ordinator for large-scale capital projects. Think through how you would respond to the following questions:

- How would you describe yourself?
- Which aspects of yourself are most dominant at work?
- Which are your favourite roles?

Companies have identities, too, and these give employees and customers a clear idea of what to expect from them. Where there is a strong figurehead as founder, that person often incorporates their identity and values into the organization. Take care to check that the external identity that attracts you to an organization is applied to the staff, too. For example, it would be inconsistent of an educational organization to advocate strongly the importance of lifelong learning while blocking its staff from attending development courses for themselves.

What kind of organization do you want to work with?

You should work on a snappy response to this question. Think more broadly than *I want to work in pharmaceuticals* or *I want to work in retailing* as there are many companies to choose from. What differentiates them surrounds the *how* questions – the way in which they achieve their objectives.

I want to work in a company that recognizes and rewards a job well done.

Values

Your values relate to what is important to you when you are at work. A key value might be security. If this describes you, then an organization with a low staff turnover and a good pension may suit you. If you value variety, then a job that sends you around the world to buy products may appeal to you. It may be that what matters most to you is a sense of 'celebrity', and so the opportunity to represent your organization at a national level would be exciting and stimulating. Conversely, if this doesn't fit, you will be thrown into panic, anxiety or sheer terror at the thought of working in that environment. Think through the answers to the following questions:

- What matters to you when you are at work?
- Why do you go to work?

Whatever your values, you will enjoy your job much more if they are matched at work.

Preferred environment

The comfort and safety of your surroundings and the people you are with make a big difference to job satisfaction and achievement. Think about what effect different work environments have had on you and which aspects you would like in any future jobs. Is it important to be able to work in natural light or more significant to have your own desk or office? You may also want to consider any environmental factors, such as transport, housing and schooling which affect you and your family.

Now you have a clear idea of what you are looking for in a job, you can start to form some answers to the following questions.

Why do you want to work for us? What makes you think you're right for the job? What makes this the right job for you?

...*I want to work for an organization that is committed to staff involvement at all levels. I know that you have installed a rigorous 360-degree appraisal scheme and that you have acted positively on the feedback you have received.*

...*When I rang your department for the annual figures, I was impressed by the response from the person I spoke to. I rang back for some fairly obscure data and felt that my request was treated seriously. That is just one example of the way I like to deal with people. I feel I would fit into this organization.*

In the examples above, you are reinforcing how you do your job by talking about what you know about the organization. In a very subtle way, you have communicated aspects of yourself. At the same time, with this as with the following question, we would always advocate honesty.

What is most important to you in a job? What would make the ideal employer for you?

The most important aspect of a job is that I am able to work at my own pace and in my own space. I am a specialist in my commercial field and I have learned over the years to trust my intuition. My work is highly regarded throughout the industry and I wish to stay pre-eminent. It follows that my ideal employer would be someone prepared to nurture my creativity and appreciate my need for space. I enjoy working in organizations where my thoroughness is valued and appreciated.

What is your management style?

Management style has changed over the last decade. There are many terms used to describe management style, including the following:

● Coaching – let's find a solution together
● Empowering – working through others to develop their responsibility and accountability
● Quality – focused on how we can improve
● Customer-focused listening, understanding, responding to both customers and markets

For most organizations, language such as 'Do as I say' is now abhorrent. Change is something that is embraced rather than opposed, and the quality of working relationships is seen as the key to achievement. From your research, you should have some idea about the organization's style of management:

● How do they describe their management style?
● What do they refer to in their competencies?
● What do you pick up through their literature?

It is quite normal to have a series of questions about your management style. However, interviewers are not interested in your theoretical perspective but how you put the theory into practice. So prepare your answers. If you talk about empowerment, tell them how you do it and with what results.

What kind of people do you find it difficult to work with? How have you worked successfully with these difficult people?

Watch out for these! There could be an assumption that you have some difficulties in your people management skills. It would be foolish to suggest that you never have challenges with people. Here you need to demonstrate tact, understanding and diplomacy without being sidetracked into a lengthy discussion of certain types of people.

Everyone had lost patience with one member of the team who always came up with why something wasn't good enough or couldn't possibly work. When I spent some time with her and told her that it appeared as if she was always putting our ideas down, she was horrified. She explained that she thought the team was working brilliantly and she wanted to use her attention to detail as a final hurdle. We agreed that she would point out all the positives she associated with our projects and we would give her five minutes at the end of every team meeting to air her concerns. After that no one could have hoped for a more committed team member.

You have been given a project that required you to interact at different levels within the organization. How do you do this? What levels are you most comfortable with?

This is a two-part question that probes communication and self-confidence. The first part indirectly asks how you interact with senior staff and motivate those working with and for you on a project. The second part of the question is saying: *Tell me whom you regard as your peer group – help me categorize you.*

Which management thinker has influenced your practice?

Be honest with this question. If the answer is 'no one' then state it. You may not be a great reader but something will have influenced your practice. You could interpret this question and talk about a manager you respect.

I have been most influenced by ... Their work had the most significant effect on my understanding of how I could make a difference and how I always needed to have my goal in mind.

I am not a great reader of management books. I have worked for many people who have influenced my practice, and through observation and discussion I have come to understand what goes on in their heads, and I have applied this to myself.

You may also be asked for your definitions of terms such as: 'co-operation', 'management', etc. You should have some definitions up your sleeve for this type of question. Avoid sounding textbook-based and wherever possible give examples.

Are you a natural-born leader?

Some of us are natural leaders and you will know if you are. Natural-born leaders are chosen for the role of management and leadership because of their ability to manage complex situations and lead teams and individuals. They possess natural leadership qualities and enthusiasm and confidence. Their staff trust and believe in them. They will go the extra mile willingly for a natural leader.

When answering this question, you need to build on examples that demonstrate this. You could also use examples outside work to show the naturalness of your leadership: 'captain of my tennis club'; 'voted to represent my team at a national event'. Whatever you choose to say, make sure that your leadership qualities stand out.

What motivates you?

Questions about motivation are trying to uncover which forces determine what you want and need from your working life. These are sometimes referred to as 'drivers' and are sources of energy and direction that become obvious as people study the shape of their working lives. Research has identified nine distinct career drivers that can act as key motivators.

Key drivers	Seeking
Power/influence	To be in control of people and resources
Affiliation	To be part of the group, being popular
Expertise	A high level of accomplishment in a specialized field
Material rewards	Possessions, wealth and a high standard of living
Creativity	To innovate and be identified with original work
Autonomy	To be independent and able to make key decisions
Security	A solid and predictable future
Search for meaning	Doing things you believe are valuable for their own sake
Status	To be recognized, admired and respected

(Adapted from Schein's career drivers)

Take some time to think about which of these have motivated you in your career choices and decisions to date. How do they fit in with the opportunities offered by the types of jobs and organizations you are considering at present? Then think about the following set of questions.

What motivates you to put in your greatest effort at work?
What are the most important rewards you want from your work?

It is important to me that my work makes a positive contribution to the wider community. I want to work on issues that are important and do more than just promoting my career.

I want my products to have my 'name' on them and I want to be genuinely innovative in my work.

What was your least favourite position? What role did your boss play in your career at that point?

Here the interviewer is trying to uncover style-related issues, how you cope with a negatively framed question and how you constructively criticize both your boss and the organization. Be careful not to lay blame.

What I disliked most about my former company was the fact that it was risk averse. It was a mature company with exceptionally low staff turnover. Working for the Sales Director had the most challenges. We worked very well together personally, but he needed to be much more proactive in terms of anticipating the workload. He prided himself in putting out fires. My style, conversely, was to forecast potential problems before they arose. It got very tiring after a while and took most of the fun out of coming to work every day.

What is more important to you, pay or the type of job you are doing?

If you are applying for a job with a high element of commission, then you will do well with a 'materials reward' driver. If you are going for a more vocational type of job, then 'search for meaning' or 'affiliation' is likely to be stronger.

Summary

Today we have taken you through the questions relating to 'how you do the job'. We have given you some exercises to help you clarify and understand what matters to you at work and how you have achieved this in the past. You may be fascinated by the information you gain. Use these insights to frame your answers and also to check your compatibility with the organization and whether the role matches your expectations.

Why this job?

- Identity – who am I or who do I want to be?
- Values – what matters to me in a job and in my work?
- Environment – where do I want to work and who do I want to work with?

What is your management style?

- Your theoretical understanding
- Examples of good practice

What motivates you?

- Your driving forces

Interviewers want to understand the strategies and styles you employ when managing yourself and others. They want to know what drives you to do the work you do.

SUNDAY MONDAY TUESDAY WEDNESDAY THURSDAY FRIDAY SATURDAY

Fact-check (answers at the back)

Some of these questions have more than one correct answer.

1. How would you answer the question *Why do you want the job?*
   a) Because I'm out of work ❏
   b) I was excited by the role ❏
   c) It matches my skills ❏
   d) I'm ready for a move ❏

2. In saying why you want the job, how should you sound?
   a) Prepared ❏
   b) Desperate ❏
   c) Proactive ❏
   d) Considered ❏

3. How should you describe yourself?
   a) By your characteristics ❏
   b) By your role ❏
   c) In terms of the organization you work for ❏
   d) In terms of your profession ❏

4. If your key driver were affiliation, what would this mean?
   a) You need security ❏
   b) You need autonomy ❏
   c) You need a tidy office ❏
   d) You need to be popular ❏

5. How should you answer a question about your management style?
   a) Talk about theory, not practice ❏
   b) Talk about practice, not theory ❏
   c) Give examples of how you manage people ❏
   d) Show that you are an authoritarian ❏

6. How should you describe your style?
   a) By using feedback, what others have said about you ❏
   b) By relating it to the company competencies ❏
   c) By reflecting the words used in the company brochures ❏
   d) By talking about yourself from a theoretical perspective ❏

7. In talking about who influences your career, who should you refer to?
   a) Your manager ❏
   b) Nobody ❏
   c) A significant family member ❏
   d) An inspirational leader ❏

8. In answering a question about rewards in your career, what should you refer to?
   a) Money ❏
   b) Achievements ❏
   c) Recognition ❏
   d) Promotion ❏

9. In describing what influenced your least favourite time at work, what should you describe?
   a) Your manager ❏
   b) A challenging situation ❏
   c) Challenging market conditions ❏
   d) A difficult team you inherited ❏

10. If your key driver were search for meaning, what would this mean?
a) You need to have fun ❏
b) Doing things you believe are valuable for their own sake ❏
c) You need to be admired and respected ❏
d) You need to be in control ❏

SUNDAY
MONDAY
TUESDAY
WEDNESDAY
THURSDAY
FRIDAY
SATURDAY

FRIDAY

Will you fit?

So you have convinced the interviewer that you can do the job. You have the necessary skills, knowledge, experience, training and, given the opportunity, your behaviours, motivators, style and characteristics would help you do the job. The important question now is *Will you fit?*

Today, we will focus on convincing the interviewer that you will. The question of *fit* is being assessed from your very first exchange: from the style and language in your letter or application, your choice of clothes, through to your degree of articulation and your understanding of the role and the organization, and to how you respond to their questions.

It may be useful for you to reflect on how you judge *fit* for yourself. How do you know when a relationship, a role or a decision is right? While we often make big decisions in our lives on the basis of them matching certain criteria, there is also a strong element of fit, intuition or something simply feeling right – a gut reaction. While this is, to some degree, a subconscious process, it is probably the most influential in decision making.

Today we will cover scenarios and the following questions:

- How long will you stay?
- How much are you worth?
- How do you fit this role?
- How does the role fit you?

The importance of fit

This is a key area for the interviewer to get right. In the main, they want to recommend the appointment of someone who will benefit the organization, work well with the existing staff and embrace the culture. Sometimes, of course, they want just the opposite. You may be applying for a job that involves reducing staffing and making a team leaner and more efficient. If that is so, make sure it fits you.

The interviewer needs to achieve a good fit between the job role and the organization's expectations; someone with the personal and professional ability that matches the organization's policies and management style. The better the fit, the more harmonious and effective the professional relationship will be.

The interviewer's objectives	The interviewee's objectives
To have positive answers to these questions:	To answer yes to these questions:
● Do you fit the company image?	● Would I feel proud to be with this company?
● How will you adapt to the culture?	● Will I want to talk about where I work?
● Would our clients want you at their meetings?	● Will I wear the uniform with pride?
● Will you blend with the team?	● Do I feel comfortable here?
● Could you represent us?	● Could I represent them?

These are probably the most important questions for the interviewer to find answers to. A wrong decision can be costly to the organization in terms of time, energy, lost opportunities, and internal and external relationship problems. This is the final balancing act for the interviewer.

You must have been exposed to someone in your career who didn't fit, so you will understand at first hand what this feels like and the disruption it can cause. Therefore, the judgement of fit is the part of the interview process that interviewers are most cautious about. There are some sophisticated questions and situations that have been devised to gauge fit, but much of this part of the process remains instinctive. Decisions are often made on a 'gut' reaction or discussions that rest on perception rather than evidence. If there is ever a part of the process that interviewers will discuss at length, disagree on and even get second opinions on, it is fit.

In some cases it is obvious: the interviewer will know immediately whether you will fit. Sometimes they make comments such as:

- 'There was something about them ...'
- 'I'm sure they could do the job ...'
- 'I can't put my finger on it ...'
- 'I'm not sure how they would fit ...'

Case history

One of the companies we advised was receiving many complaints about the style and attitude of a senior manager. He was rude and unfeeling, with no interest in his team's concerns. When he was employed, this organization was overstaffed and running at a loss. He was brought in to stop the downward spiral. There was no room for sentiment and he achieved his objectives. However, once this goal was achieved it was more important to retain people. His style was not consistent with motivating and encouraging people. Eventually, he moved on to another 'troubleshooting' job. He no longer fitted in and rather than change his style, he changed job – a pattern that would repeat itself throughout his career.

As fit is so difficult to gauge, companies have devised their own sets of questions to help uncover whether your style, manner, character and values match theirs.

Today is all about helping you to demonstrate that you *fit* the organization and helping you decide whether they *fit* with you and your aspirations for the future.

Scenarios

Increasingly, interviewers are making use of real-life, relevant situations to check how you fit with their organization. Most of the colleagues we talked to agreed that their most challenging and revealing questions were ones which asked the candidate to declare how they would react in a given scenario. 'What would you do?' questions can fall into two categories: hypothetical or real. They focus on how you would cope. The interviewer does not want to hear the answer *it depends* – they already know that. They want to know how you process information, what your first actions would be; who you would talk to ... the list goes on. You have to think on your feet and put yourself in the interviewer's shoes. The context of their question should give you some understanding of what are they interested in, so you can respond with that in mind.

> **It's 8.00 a.m., your most prestigious client is due to arrive at 9.00 a.m. and the computer equipment for your presentation hasn't arrived. What do you do?**
>
> *I think we've all faced situations like this. I always try to plan against anything like this happening by setting up presentations in advance and not leaving things to chance. But given this situation, I would have the contact numbers for the people bringing the equipment. Then I could contact them and, if necessary, arrange for other equipment to be delivered.*

'What would you do?' questions often bring a similar level of anxiety as the real situations. Don't slip into the easy trap of saying 'Panic!' in reply. You may be thinking that, and many of these situations do create a level of anxiety, but your interviewer wants to hear how you would cope, what you would do and how you would deliver, given the uncertainty and ambiguity that happens in everyday situations.

Every company has its own quirks. How dysfunctional was your last company, and how would you deal with a company's shortcomings and inconsistencies?

When we came across this question, from sample questions used by a large multinational company, it stopped us in our tracks. Remember, this is a 'What would you do?' question. Beware of these questions as they are there to test your ability to remain objective and positive about your last organization, and your interpretation of dysfunction – what it means to you, how you tackle organizational development issues. The list is endless, but your answer must remain succinct – so think carefully.

My last company was open about its dysfunctionality as it was the flip side of its effectiveness. The passion with which it attacked the business created a high degree of emotion in all functions. This led to a need to react very quickly when messages or changes were interpreted wrongly to prevent them spiralling out of control. In one case, for example, I called everyone to a meeting to explain the reason for a particular management decision. This cut down the time and energy everyone was spending on discussing it and making comment and judgement.

You are chairing the monthly interdepartmental meeting. All is going well – except for the Head of Operations, a bright and ambitious woman. She keeps looking at her watch, sighing and whispering 'hurry up' when someone else speaks. Eventually she cracks and suggests you speed the meeting up – she has places to go, people to see. What would you do?

I would want to tackle this in two ways – firstly at the meeting by acknowledging her urgency and asking for her patience to listen to all contributions. I would also remind her of our agreed timings and that we would finish on time. My next step would be to talk to her alone outside the meeting, challenge her behaviour and ask for her ideas about reaching a workable solution.

Your success in answering all the 'What would you do?' questions is to think about the interviewer's objectives and respond to these directly. Be honest, succinct, direct and help them understand how this relates to you generally.

 By putting forward a scenario and asking what you would do if faced with it, the interviewer is hoping to find out how you would deal with the unexpected and how you might respond in the real world where not everything goes according to plan.

The other forms of scenario question ask you about a current situation, such as:

What do you think of the current government's approach to ...?
How do you think the credit crunch could have been averted ...?
Compare the leadership of Barack Obama with another world leader.

There are many reasons for questions such as this. Firstly, the interviewer is interested in whether you take an interest in what goes on in the world. Also, your answer is likely to give the interviewer an insight into your values, which may help them to understand whether these fit with the values of the organization. This is not an opportunity to present a detailed political opinion but to demonstrate to the interviewer that you are informed and see all sides of a debate.

How long will you stay?

While interviewers have a current need, they will also be thinking about the future. The investment in the interview process or in consultant costs needs to demonstrate some return. So the questions which relate to how long you will stay or what you want to do next are important to the interviewer. A good fit is likely to encourage you to stay, and be a greater return on the investment.

How long will you stay with the organization?

If the interviewer asks this question, they may be thinking of offering you a job. So build on this. You may want to end your answer with a question of your own that really puts the ball back in the interviewer's court.

I would really like an opportunity to make a contribution to the success of the organization and could see where I could add value. I can operationalize strategies and love to learn. As long as I am growing professionally and challenged, there is no reason for me to make a move. How long do you think I would be challenged here?

You've only been with your current employer for a short time.

As we mentioned previously, the recruitment process is a long and costly one. When recruitment agencies are appointed their fee can be as much as 30 per cent of your first year's annual package. The last thing any employer wants is to appoint someone who is only going to stay for a short period of time. You will need to reassure the interviewer that this is not a pattern.

Yes, I realize that this may make you cautious of me, but I've found that I need to move on to gain more experience and really challenge myself. I think I can achieve this in your organization and I feel I am ready to settle down in a new role such as this.

You have been with your employer a long time – why?

There could be many reasons why you've shown loyalty to your existing employer. It may be that you liked your job, the people, or that the environment was changing so much there was always challenge and opportunity. Respond truthfully, but do bring attention to this as demonstrating loyalty and commitment, which are core parts of you.

Where do you see yourself in ten years' time?

Questions such as this don't require you to make a long-term commitment to the organization. They are probing your career ambitions and goals. Most managers would be expected to have thought through their career plans so that they could at least articulate a goal, although it is surprising how few can. This question is difficult to answer in terms of a role, but it's not asking that. It's asking you to consider where you see yourself in terms of responsibilities, contribution to an organization, work style and so on.

Ten years ought to give me time to grow within an organization like yours, which provides the right training, challenge and management. I am ambitious and would be keen to reach my full potential, which would be ...

You may want to add: *It is reasonable to expect that other exciting opportunities will crop up in the meantime and I am always keen to apply my skills in different environments.*
The question may also be asked in the following way:

How would this post fit into your long-term career plans?

You may want to answer along these lines:

My plans have always been influenced by experiences and opportunities. I believe this post would be just right. I could use the skills I have developed and be sufficiently challenged to develop while learning from new people, processes and clients. I could then look forward to what opportunities my success in this role would bring.

 If you are too staged in your responses, your interviewer will detect this. The words you use need to be yours, not ours, or they will sound unconvincing.

How much are you worth?

It is not uncommon to be asked to put a price on your head.
You can quantify worth in many ways:

- the value you add
- your market value
- what you are paid at the moment
- how much the organization is prepared to pay.

Our advice would be start with a high figure and don't be afraid
of negotiation. Many people find they undersell themselves
because they are not ready for such a direct question, so
don't fall into that trap. Be bold. It is not unreasonable to ask
for 10–20 per cent more than your current package – always
quantify all your benefits: discounts, healthcare, pension, car
allowance, shares, and so on when negotiating salary, as these
could be worth more than you imagine.

What salary do you require?

I am looking for something in the range of £x–£y.

You don't need to go into any more detail than this. Do not
answer this question with a question, such as *How much are
you prepared to pay?*

How do you fit this role?

You may be faced with questions you feel are only asked of you because of your gender, disability, ethnicity or sexual orientation. These are some of the more difficult questions to deal with as they challenge your fit, not on the basis of skills, experience or behaviour but because of who you are. The key to these questions is to understand the reason they are asked.

In the interviewee's seat it may feel as if you are being discriminated against; in the interviewer's seat it may be that they genuinely want to know if you are a good person in whom to invest their time, training and money.

Keeping the interviewer's underlying question in mind, you will have some guidelines on how to answer. If you want the job, then you have to answer the question in a way that says: *Yes, I am a good bet or a low risk.*

This style of question is disappearing, but every so often you will be faced with one that can 'wobble' you, not just for the duration of the question but beyond. You may also want to consider whether you would want to work for an employer that asks such questions as:

- What is your marital status?
- Are you in a long-term relationship?
- Who do you live with?
- Do you plan to have a family? When?
- How many children do you have?
- What are your childcare arrangements?

What are your childcare arrangements?

In response to this question, you may choose to say:

If you are asking would I be willing and able to travel as needed by the job, the answer is 'yes'. I would just need some notice to make the necessary arrangements ... I am willing to work overtime and have often stayed late to complete tasks.

This can come across better than a direct: *Would you ask that question of a man?*

Also, don't be surprised if you are asked for your birth certificate, passport, proof of qualifications, or any document containing your national insurance number. Legislation requires employers to establish that every employee, at whatever level, can legally work in the country.

How does the role fit you?

The last time you bought a car or a house, did you ask about the financing, have it valued or investigate its reliability? We would hope that you did! We would suggest that your next career move is at least as important. So if you want to impress your potential manager with your grasp of the position and knowledge of the organization, it makes sense to draw up a list of questions. Asking good questions at an interview helps you get the information you need to make an intelligent decision; it also shows the interviewer that you've done your homework and are in a position to discuss the job's potential opportunities and challenges. Here are just a few questions you may want to think of asking:

Asking about the organization

- What is the five-year plan for the organization?
- I consider your competitors to be ... what do you think?
- What did you wish you knew about the organization before you started?
- What values are sacred to the organization?
- How are decisions made?
- What is the organization's philosophy towards employees?

Asking about success and measurement

- Could you give me examples of the best results the previous job holders have attained?
- What is your biggest problem and what role would I have in solving it?

Asking about development opportunities

● What opportunities of advancement are there for me?
● Why did this post become vacant?

Asking about the role

● What are your key selection criteria for the post?
● How long have you worked here? In what capacities?
● How do you allocate and review work?

TIP *Asking articulate and well-thought-through questions leaves a good impression on your interviewer. It's a great opportunity to professionally challenge the interviewer and be remembered.*

Try to avoid going over old information and remember that this is not the appropriate place to talk through terms and conditions – this leaves the interviewer with the impression that this is all you are interested in. The interviewer wants to know that you are taking the process seriously and have done the necessary preparation to convince them to offer you the job.

Summary

Today we have addressed the issue of *fit*. The interviewer wants to find out whether you are the right person for the job, not just in terms of what you can do but how you do it. This can be a tricky area to prepare for, as so much around fit is not articulated. But we recommend reading company literature and paying attention to all the descriptions of the role. Everyone you meet will give you an impression of the organization and they will be good barometers of fit. Organizations don't want clones; they want people who uniquely contribute but match the values of the organization and the culture.

● How could you fit into their current team?
● Are you a worthwhile investment?
● Does the role and organization meet your aspirations?

It's important to remember that the interview process is also about assessing whether the organization fits your needs and aspirations.

So far this week, we have developed your understanding of how to respond to tough interview questions tackling the issues of how you present your career, yourself and how you will do the job. Tomorrow, we will help you put the finishing touches to your preparation by focusing on your readiness for the interview questions to come.

Fact-check (answers at the back)

Some of these questions have more than one correct answer.

1. How will your fit into the organization and role be judged?
   a) By your research ❑
   b) By the words you use ❑
   c) By your choice of clothes ❑
   d) By your handshake ❑

2. What does the interviewer want to find out?
   a) Would clients want you at their meetings? ❑
   b) Will you fit with the team? ❑
   c) Do you have a sense of humour? ❑
   d) How will you adapt to the culture? ❑

3. When asked what you would do in a given scenario, how should you respond?
   a) It depends ❑
   b) Talk to all the stakeholders ❑
   c) Look at the data ❑
   d) Get the customer perspective ❑

4. How should you respond to questions about whether your previous company was dysfunctional?
   a) Very ❑
   b) In parts ❑
   c) As dysfunctional as any company ❑
   d) Where do you want me to start? ❑

5. When asked how long you will stay, how should you answer?
   a) As long as you'll have me ❑
   b) As long as I add value ❑
   c) Until I retire ❑
   d) Until the role lacks challenge ❑

6. What is the purpose of a question asking where you see yourself in ten years' time?
   a) To require you to make a long-term commitment ❑
   b) To probe your career ambitions and goals ❑
   c) To satisfy the interviewer's curiosity ❑
   d) To assess your sense of responsibility and your potential contribution ❑

7. If asked how much you think you are worth, how should you answer?
   a) £....,000 ❑
   b) What would you be prepared to pay? ❑
   c) More than my current package ❑
   d) This is the value I'd add ❑

8. When asked what you believe to be a discriminatory question, how would you respond?
   a) Would you ask that of a man/woman? ❑
   b) Are you asking ...? ❑
   c) Why are you asking me that question? ❑
   d) Positively – simply answering the question ❑

9. What sorts of question should you ask?
a) What is the package? ❏
b) What did you wish you knew about the organization when you started? ❏
c) How are decisions made? ❏
d) What would success look like in the role? ❏

10. Why should you ask questions?
a) To suggest that you've done your homework ❏
b) To challenge the interviewer ❏
c) To recap old information ❏
d) To leave a good impression ❏

SUNDAY

MONDAY

TUESDAY

WEDNESDAY

THURSDAY

FRIDAY

SATURDAY

SATURDAY

Are you ready?

At this stage of the week, you should be feeling more confident about tackling tough interview questions. Only you know what it takes to build your confidence and it's a fine balance between acceptable and unacceptable confidence. It's important that you are able to control your nerves, so they don't get in the way of you giving a good impression.

We have attempted to prepare you by looking at the interview from different perspectives. Perhaps the most important perspective is to put yourself in the shoes of the interviewer, to understand their motives for asking the questions, and to respond appropriately. Remember, your interviewer thinks you can do the job and they want to help you bring your application to life.

Today is about bringing all your preparation together and harnessing all your inner resources to ensure that you are ready and raring to go when you are invited to your next interview.

Today we will cover the following aspects of interview preparation:

- Rehearsing your responses
- Preparing your thoughts
- Focusing on your outcome
- Relaxing before the event
- Is this the job for you?

Rehearsing your responses

We have focused throughout the week on your responses to tough interview questions. Preparing what you are going to say and how you are going to say it are equally important.

Have you ever been in a situation in which you've wanted to listen to someone because they know their subject or you respect their opinions? Try as you might, you've been unable to give them your full attention. Their delivery has undermined the message. This could happen to you, too. You can prevent this happening by spending time rehearsing. Prepare yourself so that every aspect of what you say convinces and engages your audience.

TO GET THE JOB OR NOT TO GET THE JOB?

Case history

We once came across a very able applicant for a role, who for the first ten minutes was so nervous that she couldn't maintain eye contact or listen to the questions. She managed to get over this and her preparation helped. She referred to examples she had brought with her and managed to control her nervousness – she got the job!

Keep in mind these objectives:

- Get myself as ready as I can.
- Put all my preparation into practice.
- Imagine and rehearse my success.
- Draw on and recognize all my resources.

Success at interview depends on your readiness. Be sure not to cram so much into your week that you are overly tired, or so absorbed in preparing for a presentation that you forget to spend time preparing for the interview itself. And always give yourself enough time to get to the interview itself.

Practice, feedback and learning

What makes a great performance? Whatever the context in which you practise sport, art, craft or business, there are some essential components: skill, understanding the criteria for success, practice and learning. The interview is just the same. While our comments this week have focused on developing your skills and understanding the criteria for success, do not underestimate the importance of practice, feedback and learning.

Saying your responses out loud, asking a trusted friend to be your interviewer, working with a coach and recording yourself can all help. Physically saying the words will give you a sense of their impact, as some of your answers may look better than they sound! Rehearsal takes planning and effort, so give yourself time and don't be put off by the fact that it may be embarrassing. It's better to be embarrassed in front of a colleague or friend, where the cost is personal, than in front of the interviewer, where the cost may include prospects and earning potential. 'The more I practise the luckier I get' was **the** response golfer Gary Player made to a shout of 'Lucky shot!'

Often, a bad experience, when broken down into its component parts, does not seem so bad after all. A bad experience may affect you and it can leave you expecting the worst to happen. This can send your self-esteem plummeting, with far-reaching consequences. If you're struggling with some of these thoughts, you need to exorcize them by exposing them to the light of rational thought.

TIP *Balance your thoughts on what could go wrong with what will go right. When you think positively, you behave positively and it shows.*

Answering the following questions may help your rehearsal:

	Worst interview to date	Best interview to date
How did you prepare?		
What did you feel about the job?		
What did you notice on arrival?		
What did you do well?		
What could you have done differently?		

Preparing your thoughts

Many of our comments this week have been based on logical, practical and analytical assumptions. Some commentators refer to this as 'left brain' activity. While it's likely that much of an interview will also be based there, remember the other side, your right brain activity. This is the source of your imagination and creativity. Your ability to demonstrate your creativity is important to your success. It's part of your uniqueness. You can also harness your imagination to create the interview in which you feel at your best.

Believe in yourself

Think for a moment about the notion of beginner's luck. No one has told them how difficult it is to succeed and they have no prior memory of doing it well or badly. In fact, if they believe in beginner's luck, they will expect to do well the first time. Then, depending on their beliefs, they go on and build on their success – or they become gradually worse. Our ability to achieve excellence or perform well is dependent on how well we believe we can do.

What poor performers say	What good performers say
• It was a fluke.	• I can make this a success.
• It won't last.	• I can keep doing this well.
• I always mess up.	• I always do well.

You can make or break an interview just by talking to yourself in one or other of the ways listed above. You know what you should say to yourself and how to mentally prepare yourself for the task ahead. We would recommend the following:

- Encourage yourself.
- Tell yourself you can do it.
- Think about previous successes.
- Focus on what success could bring.

It may help you to develop affirmations: short, positive statements that introduce and reinforce the way you want to be. They should always be stated in the present or present continuous tense, as if they already exist. They work on the premise that thoughts create experience and keep the mind programmed in the positive. As you repeat them regularly, so you will believe them and your mind will focus on what you want.

Writing affirmations

Here are some examples of positive affiirmations:

- I always do well at interview.
- I enjoy the opportunity to tackle tough interview questions.
- Every day brings a new and welcome challenge.

 Write and repeat your own affirmations about the interview and the new post you are aiming for.

Also remind yourself that the interviewer doesn't hold all the trump cards. Put yourself in their shoes and you'll realize that they have as much at stake in the interview as you. What if they appoint the wrong person? They are probably under as much pressure as you are because they can't afford to make a bad decision.

Focusing on your outcome

There are examples from many walks of life that suggest that if you focus on your outcome and imagine yourself having succeeded or being successful, you will achieve whatever you set out to achieve. Setting goals focuses your attention and action. With clear goals, you are more likely to engage in purposeful behaviour. When you know what you want, you are more likely to pursue it. With realistic and specific goals, you know what you are aiming for; with no goals, you have no target.

So start this process by thinking what you want your outcome to be and create some affirmations to achieve it.

Exercise

Find a place where you can sit or lie down for a few uninterrupted minutes.

1 Close your eyes and create your ideal interview.

2 Start from the night before. See and feel yourself relaxed and sleeping well.

3 Wake up feeling energetic and keen to be there.

4 Imagine yourself arriving for the interview.

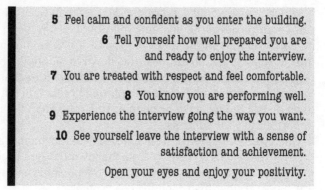

5 Feel calm and confident as you enter the building.

6 Tell yourself how well prepared you are and ready to enjoy the interview.

7 You are treated with respect and feel comfortable.

8 You know you are performing well.

9 Experience the interview going the way you want.

10 See yourself leave the interview with a sense of satisfaction and achievement.

Open your eyes and enjoy your positivity.

Relaxing before the event

We would encourage everyone reading this book to take or create some form of relaxation before an interview. How you relax is your choice. You will know what works for you. For some this may mean activity: a visit to the gym, swimming, a round of golf, gardening, walking the dog. For others it may mean inactivity, stopping the round of activities which make up a normal day and spending time with family, friends or partners; or taking time on your own to read, listen to music, write letters or do nothing. What matters is that you do something that relaxes you.

You also need to decide how you approach the interview, otherwise all your relaxation will be in vain. Picture the two scenes below:

Scene 1	Scene 2
● Work until midnight the night before	● Complete preparation the previous day
● Haven't received a map	● Ring to check location
● Decide to set off, will ring on approach	● Decide to travel by train
● Arrive in town with just 15 minutes to spare	● Plan to arrive with an hour to spare
● Car park is a 10-minute walk	● Have lunch on site
● There is a queue at security of 20 people	● Meet employees, talk about the company

SUNDAY | MONDAY | TUESDAY | WEDNESDAY | THURSDAY | FRIDAY | SATURDAY

111

Which scene would you prefer? Just reading Scene 1 can raise your anxiety. Imagine how you would fare walking into an interview with that as your build-up. Creating your own Scene 2 is not about luck; it is down to planning and preparation. If you want to do well, don't leave it to chance! Part of your preparation is leaving time to relax and not to be distracted by tasks or people. This relaxation time is important to your success.

When you are relaxed and not tired, you are much more able to deal with situations as they emerge. You are much less likely to make mistakes because you will be alert. Your words and actions will support rather than contradict each other.

Is this the job for you?

As we saw yesterday, the fit issue affects both parties. You may be ideal for the company, but are they the perfect match for you?

Will they:

● support your development?
● offer good prospects for the future?
● fit with your style?
● offer a job that is sufficiently challenging?

How will you:

● complement the team?
● add value?

If your answers to any of the above questions are not clear, then you should check your goals and motivation. One of the major factors that can influence whether the job is for you will be your relationship with your boss. We would recommend that you never accept a position without an interview with your immediate manager. No one has more impact on your career. Their performance, feedback, attitude, expectations and style will have an effect on your performance and the way you feel about your job. In turn, their conversations with their boss can colour higher management's long-term perceptions of you.

Get to know your boss

Before you accept a job, get to know your boss. Ask them probing questions:

- What are the key indicators of success for you in this role?
- What do you expect from me personally?
- How could I influence you?
- How would I know your opinion of my performance?
- How would you describe your style?

You need to determine whether your work styles, goals and philosophies are compatible. Decide whether this is someone you could admire. If they prove not to be, perhaps you should look for another job, managed by a person who more closely mirrors your image of a good manager.

Understand the company's values

By reading company literature, and by active listening, you can uncover what their values are. By looking at images or examples used when answering your questions, you will get a feel for how the company likes to see itself.

TIP *If you find yourself at variance with your potential employer's value system, you would do well to consider any job offer very carefully.*

It is difficult to be successful in a culture in which you feel an outsider. If you sense that the fit is not right from your perspective, then we would suggest that you don't pursue the opportunity. If the company is embarking on a major change, be sure of where the motivation and commitment for the change comes from. Are you being appointed as one of the change agents? There is nothing more de-skilling than being in a company where you don't fit and there should be signs of this almost immediately. If your gut reaction tells you no, listen to it and try to analyse why.

Practicalities

If you think you are close to a job offer that you want to accept, this may be the time to talk about the practicalities. Even if you don't discuss these in the interview, they are worth considering when you are negotiating from the strong position of having a job offer.

Practicalities may include finding out the following:

● Will you need a medical?
● Preferred start date
● Pension details
● Salary and benefits
● Private healthcare scheme
● Expected job and company growth
● Development opportunities
● Potential career paths
● Annual leave
● Profit sharing
● Induction

So, now you are fully prepared, you've thought through your responses and have practised how to deliver them. You have done your research on the role and the organization and you should have replaced any anxiety you had with excitement about the process.

Summary

An interview is a discussion with a clear purpose: the interviewer wants to know how you will bring benefits to them and the company. They are seeking someone who can fill a vacancy with minimum upheaval and maximum impact.

You want a new job, a new challenge or a change. You also want to get there as calmly as possible.

Our advice throughout the week relates to the preparation and thought required to develop a script for your answers. But remember to think of your interview as a discussion rather than a test. Even if a panel of people interview you, they are only asking one question at a time. That is what you need to concentrate on.

- Identify your tough questions.
- Establish rapport with everyone you meet.
- Describe your education, skills and competencies.
- Show your personality, what makes you tick and what matters to you in your work.
- Prepare creatively.

We wish you well in whatever types of interview you attend. You can now go to them knowing you are prepared, with all the resources you need to answer whatever you are asked. Now you've read the book, you should be saying:

'Tough questions? I don't know what you mean!'

SUNDAY
MONDAY
TUESDAY
WEDNESDAY
THURSDAY
FRIDAY
SATURDAY

Fact-check (answers at the back)

Some of these questions have more than one correct answer.

1. How should you get ready for an interview?
a) Rehearse your responses ❑
b) Relax ❑
c) Think of yourself in the role ❑
d) Do nothing ❑

2. Why should you rehearse for an interview?
a) To fill the time beforehand ❑
b) To feel embarrassed ❑
c) To set me up for success ❑
d) To help me see where I need to improve ❑

3. When thinking about interviews, what should you focus on?
a) What can go wrong ❑
b) The toughest questions ❑
c) All your responses ❑
d) How soon it will end ❑

4. How often should you reflect on interviews?
a) Sometimes ❑
b) After each one ❑
c) Never ❑
d) Only if it's not gone wrong ❑

5. How should you prepare your thoughts?
a) By imagining the worst-case scenario ❑
b) By telling yourself you can do it ❑
c) By thinking about successes ❑
d) By focusing on what success could bring ❑

6. You should expect your interviewer to be what?
a) Prepared ❑
b) Under no pressure ❑
c) Clear about the skills required ❑
d) Able to make a decision ❑

7. When attending interviews, what should your goals be?
a) To be successful ❑
b) To get through it ❑
c) To outsmart the interviewer ❑
d) To present yourself well ❑

8. How should you relax before the interview?
a) Some activity or exercise ❑
b) Walking ❑
c) Stopping what you normally do ❑
d) Working until midnight preparing the night before ❑

9. How will you know the job is for you?
a) It feels right ❑
b) It will look good on my CV ❑
c) It's challenging ❑
d) I like the people ❑

10. Nearing a job offer, which practicalities should you ask about?
a) Salary/benefits ❑
b) Will you need a medical ❑
c) Profit share ❑
d) Car parking ❑

7 × 7

1 Seven key ideas

- **Understand which are your tough questions.** Where do you stumble and what do you find difficult to answer? Sometimes even the simplest questions, such as 'Can you tell me a little about yourself?' can be tough.

- **Develop strong answers to questions about yourself.**

- **No question needs to be tough if you are well prepared.** For the interviewer, asking the right questions is the key to finding the right person for the role and there is no margin for error.

- **Feel confident.** Everyone has different ways of building their confidence. You can enhance your confidence by acknowledging your skills and what you've achieved to date and remembering other times when you've felt supremely confident.

- **Let the interviewer know you can do the job.** The interviewer must already believe you can do the job; that's why they are interviewing you. You should therefore use this opportunity to confirm it by telling the interviewer about your experience and your achievements to prove them right.

- **Respond skilfully.** How you respond to questions will distinguish you from the competition. This could include making your responses just the right length and with the right content – creatively highlighting how you would contribute to the organization.

- **Practise your answers beforehand.** This may at first take you out of your comfort zone, so rehearse your responses until you feel comfortable with them. 'You only get one chance to make a first impression', so it's imperative that you get this right.

2 Seven of the best resources

- www.businessinsider.com/30-smart-answers-to-tough-interview-questions-2013-8?IR=T – careers and interviews advice
- theundercoverrecruiter.com/10-classic-job-interview-blunders-you-must-avoid – interactive website with some great tips
- www.myinterviewsimulator.com – website with tough questions and answers
- https://www.nationalcareersservice.direct.gov.uk – publicly funded service available nationwide for UK jobseekers
- http://www.learndirect.co.uk/improve-your-job-prospects/help-getting-job/virtual-job-interview/ – an interactive site where virtual employers ask you questions and score your responses
- www.youtube.com/ – many examples of being interviewed
- Those close to you: practise answering their tough questions.

3 Seven things to avoid

- **Insufficient research** – Your research into the organization will help you understand their culture and language and the challenges for them and you in the role.
- **Not understanding why you want the role** – It's the simplest question but it often trips people up. Make your responses authentic.
- **Not addressing what makes a question tough for you** – What has made you stumble in the past? What do you find it difficult to articulate?
- **Not answering the questions** – Listen to each question carefully and answer it by thoroughly addressing the question. Take care not to respond just with your prepared answers.

- **Not selling yourself** – This is your opportunity to blow your own trumpet.
- **Not creating tough questions for them** – The questions you ask will also create an impression.
- **Insufficient preparation of your answers** – Make plenty of time to practise saying your answers out loud.

4 Seven inspiring people

- **Max Eggert** is a psychologist, several of whose books are on the recommended reading lists of international universities. His work has stood the test of time.
- **Professor Steve Peters** is a consultant psychiatrist working in business, education, health and elite and Olympic sport. His specialist interest is in the working of the human mind and how it can reach optimum performance, in all walks of life.
- **Anthony Robbins** is one of the foremost authorities on the psychology of peak performance. He is the guru of personal, professional and organizational turnaround and he has been called one of the greatest influencers of this generation.
- **Dale Carnegie**, known as 'the arch-priest of the art of making friends', pioneered the development of personal business skills, self-confidence and motivational techniques.
- **Dr Stephen Covey** is an internationally respected leadership authority, family expert, teacher, organizational consultant and author, who dedicates his life to teaching principle-centred living and leadership to individuals, families and organizations.
- Find your own inspiration – who in your network has been successful at interview?
- Be your own inspiration!

5 Seven great quotes

- 'Accept the challenges so that you can feel the exhilaration of victory.' George S. Patton

- 'The harder I practise, the luckier I get.' Gary Player
- 'I've learned that people will forget what you said, people will forget what you did, but people will never forget how you made them feel.' Maya Angelou
- 'Your attitude, not your aptitude, will determine your altitude.' Zig Ziglar
- 'Life isn't about finding yourself. Life's about creating yourself.' George Bernard Shaw
- 'Meditate. Live purely. Be quiet. Do your work with mastery. Like the moon, come out from behind the clouds! Shine.' Buddha
- 'Keep your fears to yourself, but share your courage with others.' Robert Louis Stevenson

6 Seven things to do today

- Think about what constitutes a tough question for you.
- Be clear what success looks like in this role.
- Practise some answers – say them out loud.
- Get feedback.
- Prepare your questions.
- Put yourself in the interviewers' shoes.
- Think about how you want to be remembered. What impression do you want to leave the interviewer with and how can you achieve this?

7 Seven trends for tomorrow

- There will be different stages to the selection process and methods of selection. More of these will be conducted virtually.
- Your interviewers will gather information on you from a variety of sources. When you put your name into a search engine, what do you find?

- You will need to think about the impact you have at every stage of the interview process, not just the interview itself.
- Your success at interview will be as much about cultural fit as capability.
- Questions will get fewer and tougher.
- You will be more likely to have to demonstrate your achievements through examples, such as a portfolio or a presentation.
- People who show that they can communicate and interact effectively will command an advantage.

Answers

Sunday: 1a,b,d; 2a,c,d;
3a,b,d; 4a,d; 5a,b,d; 6 a; 7a;
8b,c,d; 9a,c;
10a,b,d

Monday: 1a; 2 all of them;
3b,d; 4a; 5d; 6a; 7a; 8a,b;
9b; 10a

Tuesday: 1a,b,c; 2a,c; 3b,c,d;
4d; 5a,c; 6b,c,d; 7c,d;
8a,c,d; 9b,c,d; 10a,c,d

Wednesday: 1a,c,d; 2b;
3a,b,c; 4a,c,d; 5b,c,d; 6 d;
7a,b,d; 8a,d; 9a,c,d; 10b,c,d

Thursday: 1b,c,d; 2a,c,d;
3a,b,d; 4d; 5 b, c; 6a,b,c;
7a,c,d; 8b,c,d; 9b,c,d; 10 b

Friday: 1a,b,c; 2a,b,d; 3b,c,d;
4b,c; 5b,d; 6b,d; 7a,d; 8b,d;
9b,c,d; 10a,d

Saturday: 1a,b,c; 2c,d; 3c;
4a,b; 5b,c,d; 6a,b,c; 7a,d;
8a,b,c; 9a,c,d; 10a,b,c

ALSO AVAILABLE IN THE 'IN A WEEK' SERIES

APPRAISALS • BRAND MANAGEMENT • BUSINESS PLANS • CONTENT MARKETING • COVER LETTERS • DIGITAL MARKETING • DIRECT MARKETING • EMOTIONAL INTELLIGENCE • FINDING & HIRING TALENT • JOB HUNTING • LEADING TEAMS • MARKET RESEARCH • MARKETING • MBA • MOBILE MARKETING • NETWORKING • OUTSTANDING CONFIDENCE • PEOPLE MANAGEMENT • PLANNING YOUR CAREER • PROJECT MANAGEMENT • SMALL BUSINESS MARKETING • STARTING A NEW JOB • TACKLING TOUGH INTERVIEW QUESTIONS • TIME MANAGEMENT

For information about other titles in the 'In A Week' series, please visit www.teachyourself.co.uk